D1233887

The NEWSPAPER HEADLINE QUIZ BOOK

THE BRITISH LIBRARY

First published in 2006
by The British Library, 96 Euston Road, London NW1 2DB
in association with the Newspaper Publishers Association

Copyright © Complete Editions 2006

All rights reserved. No part of this work may be reproduced or utilised in
any form or by any means, electronic or mechanical, including
photocopying, recording or by any information storage or retrieval system,
without prior written permission of the publisher.

Packaged by Susanna Geoghegan
Cover and design by Peter Wilkinson
Typeset by David Onyett, Publishing & Production Services, Cheltenham

ISBN 0 7123 4932 4

Printed in Malta

Contents

Introduction

Newspapers are more than simply the chroniclers of passing events. They contain a snapshot of the mood and preoccupation of a society on any given day. Unlike the more free-flowing media of television, radio and the internet, a newspaper once published remains fixed – frozen, as it were, in that moment. These publications are, as has often been said, the first drafts of history, and provide a rawness and immediacy about events that is hard to match. And it is this ability both to track events and feel the pulse of society that lies behind this book.

The *Newspaper Headline Quiz Book* takes many of the most important and striking newspaper stories of the last century or so and invites the reader to test their knowledge of the events that inspired those headlines. Often those headlines are dramatic, describing such high-profile events as war, invasion, earthquakes and terrorist outrages. Others, though, may be more reflective, reflecting breakthroughs in science, technology or perhaps popular culture. The book is helpfully divided into different self-contained themes, and as indicated the subjects covered are many and diverse. They range from glorious sporting moments of triumph to the social protests that have helped change the world, and from medical breakthroughs to literary rows, with disasters both man-made and natural making a regular appearance along the way. In every case, however, the questions are inspired and illustrated by real headlines – headlines that capture the mood and emotion of that time. The format allows readers to move around from one theme to another as they choose; though equally the quizzes can be taken in the order in which they appear. Either way, these challenging questions will test the reader's knowledge not just of the events that inspired the headlines – but of the changing face of the world itself.

This book has been published to coincide with the Front Page exhibition, that has been organised to celebrate the 150th anniversary of the Association of Newspaper Journalists, and its focus on headlines is a sharp reminder of the role newspapers play in bringing big news stories to our attention on a daily basis.

Political Scandals

1. When in 1995 Cabinet minister Jonathan Aitken announced he was to sue the *Guardian* newspaper for libel, he famously claimed he would defend himself with the 'sword of truth'. Which other metaphorical martial implement did he also say he would use?

2. Aitken was later convicted of perjury and perverting the course of justice after it was revealed that associates of the Saudi royal family had paid his bill at a hotel in Paris, contradicting his own claims. Whom did Aitken say had settled the £1,000 bill, and which was the hotel in question?

3. The investigation by journalists Bob Woodward and Carl Bernstein into the Watergate scandal was helped by an anonymous source known only as 'Deep Throat'. In 2005 the identity of Deep Throat was revealed; who was he, what position did he occupy at the time of the scandal and which well-known US publication broke the news of his identity?

4. In 1986 news emerged of the so-called Iran-Contra Affair that proved a huge embarrassment for the administration of US President Ronald Reagan. Which Central American state was linked to the scandal and what was the name of the military officer who was sacked from the National Security Council by Reagan once the affair became public?

5. An American politician was involved in a mysterious car accident on a bridge at Chappaquiddick, Massachusetts, which resulted in the death of his young female passenger and a blight on his political ambitions that has lasted to this day. What is his name? What was her name? And in which year did the accident occur?

DISGRACE

6. One of the greatest scandals in French political and social history involved a Jewish army officer named Alfred Dreyfus who at the end of the 19th century was falsely accused of leaking secrets to Germany. Who was the French writer who exposed this scandal and under which title did he write a famous open letter to the French president?

7. What was the name of the British Chancellor of the Exchequer who had to resign in 1947 after he divulged details of his Budget to a political journalist on the morning of the speech?

8. The controversial resignation honours list written by Labour Prime Minister Harold Wilson after his surprise decision to quit office in 1976 ennobled a businessman who was later jailed for fraud. What was the name of this friend, and what was his business?

9. The so-called Westland affair which hit the Thatcher government in 1986, and which involved a disagreement over how to help a struggling British helicopter manufacturing company called Westland, led to the resignation of two Cabinet ministers. The first was Defence Secretary Michael Heseltine. Who was the second and what was his position?

10. In December 1998 the Trade and Industry Secretary Peter Mandelson resigned from the Cabinet after a row over the revelation that he received a £373,000 interest-free loan to help him buy a house in Notting Hill in London. From whom had he borrowed the money?

The Guardian
Saturday June 21st 1997

Sex Scandals

1. Cecil Parkinson quit the Cabinet in 1983 – even though he had initially received the support of Prime Minister Margaret Thatcher – in the wake of revelations that he had conceived a child with his secretary Sara Keays. What position did he resign from, and what was the name of the child he had with Ms Keays?

2. In 2004 Home Secretary David Blunkett became embroiled in a scandal over his private life that eventually led to his resignation. What was the name of the married woman with whom he had an affair, what was her job – and what was the nationality of the woman's nanny whose visa application became a central feature of the whole affair?

3. What was the name of the Independent Counsel who in 1998 – already in the middle of investigations about other allegations surrounding the president – started to examine events surrounding US President Bill Clinton's relationship with White House intern Monica Lewinsky?

4. For many years the French public had no idea that their long-serving president François Mitterand had had a mistress called Anne Pingeot and that he had also fathered a daughter called Mazarine with her. In which year was this news finally made public? Was it:
a 1994
b 1995
c 1996

outrageous

5. In 1963 the then War Minister John Profumo resigned over his relationship with model Christine Keeler, who had also had an affair with a naval attaché at the Soviet Embassy in London. Who was the senior legal figure appointed to investigate the whole affair?

6. Liberal Democrat leader Paddy Ashdown was re-christened 'Paddy Pantsdown' by the *Sun* newspaper after he admitted having an affair with his secretary; Ashdown himself later conceded it was a 'brilliant' if 'dreadful' headline. In which year did this revelation occur? And in which year did he finally stand down as party leader?

7. What is the name of the notorious Hollywood madam who was jailed in 1997 and who was for a while the talk of Los Angeles because it was claimed that she had many famous celebrities among her client list?

8. It was claimed by tabloid newspapers that Cabinet minister David Mellor wore a football club strip during his extramarital encounters with actress Antonia de Sanchez, an episode that eventually led to his resignation. Which was the club whose shirt he was said to have worn? And who was the publicist who is credited with having invented this spicy detail?

9. In 1988 a well-known TV evangelist in the United States briefly resigned from his ministry after it was revealed that he had been photographed taking a prostitute to a motel in Louisiana, though she later denied that they had had sex at the time. What was his name?

10. What is the name of the woman with whom Labour politician Robin Cook had an affair and later married in 1998? What was her position at the time of their extramarital relationship? And what was the given name of his first wife?

Daily Mirror
Thursday October 6th 1983

Financial Disasters and Scandals

1. The infamous Wall Street Crash in the autumn of 1929 led to the Great Depression that hit the United States during the next decade and that also had a huge impact on economies all around the world. Who was the US president at the time? Was it:

a   Calvin Coolidge
b   Herbert Hoover
c   Franklin D Roosevelt

2. Trader Nick Leeson lost around $1.4billion while working for Barings Bank, which ultimately led to the collapse of an institution that dated back to 1762; it was later bought by Dutch company ING for a nominal £1. In which country was he working for Barings at the time?

3. Publishing tycoon Robert Maxwell died in 1991 shortly before his business empire – which included the *Daily Mirror* newspaper – collapsed. It was later discovered that he had raided the pension funds of his employees to help fund his other businesses. Where did he die?

4. On Black Monday, 19 October 1987, world stock markets recorded some of their biggest ever falls in one day, with the Dow Jones in New York plunging 22.6 per cent, while the London Stock Exchange fell by more than 26 per cent. What natural phenomenon had hit southern Britain on the previous Friday, which some believe may have contributed to the financial crisis?

5. What is the name commonly given to the collective collapse of many internet-based start-up companies in 2000 and 2001 when it became evident that they had been massively overvalued?

6. In 1974 a British architect was jailed for corruption after a court was told that he had tried to bribe public figures – including MPs and local councillors – in order to win contracts, though he insisted that he had been guilty of naivety rather than criminality. What was his name?

7. Businessman Asil Nadir created a £2billion London-based company that was one of the darlings of many investors and pundits until it spectacularly and rapidly collapsed at the beginning of the 1990s. What was the name of the company? And to which country did Nadir flee after the collapse of the business?

8. Three people were imprisoned in 1990 for their part in the share-support scandal during Guinness's £2.6billion takeover bid for rival company Distillers; the company's own value was artificially inflated to deter other bidders such as the company Argyll. Who were the three men jailed?

9. Which Chancellor of the Exchequer was reported to be overheard singing after the so-called 'Black Wednesday' of 16 September 1992 when thanks in part to currency speculators the British pound was forced out of the Exchange Rate Mechanism. And where was he heard singing?

10. Name the international bank whose British branches were shut down by the Bank of England in 1991 after it was discovered to have been a centre of massive fraud and to have undisclosed debts amounting to billions of pounds. What was the nationality of the man who founded the bank in 1972?

**Daily Mail
Friday October 25th 1929**

Rail and Road Disasters

1. Thirty-five people died when two commuter trains collided at Clapham Junction – Europe's busiest railway junction – during the morning rush hour. Most of those who died were people from the south and south-east of England travelling on their way to work. Who was the Transport Secretary who had to deal with this crisis?

2. One of the worst rail disasters in history occurred on 12 December 1917 when a military train ran down a steep incline and was derailed; in all some 543 soldiers were killed. In which country did this take place?

3. In February 1975 43 people were killed when a London Underground train crashed into a dead-end tunnel after it overshot a station platform. The cause of the crash remains a mystery; the driver – who was killed in the accident – was known to be a conscientious employee who had not taken drugs or alcohol. What was the name of the station?

4. One of the worst rail disasters in recent history occurred when two trains were destroyed while passing a natural gas pipeline that was leaking – and then exploded. At least 400 people were killed and another 600 injured on the two trains. In which country did this disaster take place and in which year?

5. On 27 May 1975 more than 30 passengers plus the driver were killed, and the remaining 13 passengers seriously injured, when a coach crashed through the parapet of a bridge near Grassington, Yorkshire – it was one of the worst road accidents in British history. What had all the passengers in common?

6. A fire at the underground station at King's Cross in London in November 1987 left 31 people dead and prompted a major overhaul of safety procedures on the underground network. What is thought to have been the most likely cause of the fire?

Tragedy

7. In the summer of 1906 a train derailed at high speed near a picturesque English cathedral city killing 28 people; it is thought the driver was trying to show that his train could go faster than that of a rival rail company that had recently set up in competition. Which city was it?

8. In March 1999 a massive fire killed 39 people in a road tunnel in Europe; such was the scale of the damage and the need for new safety measures that it was three years before it could be opened to traffic again. Under which well-known mountain is this tunnel?

9. One of the worst road accidents in history took place in a road tunnel in November 1982, when at least 176 people – and possibly up to 1,000 – died after an accident involving a fuel lorry. In which country was the tunnel? Was it:
a China
b North Korea
c Afghanistan

10. A senior judge was asked to carry out the inquiry into the train crash at Ladbroke Grove near Paddington Station in October 1999, which killed 31 people. This Scottish lawyer had already carried out inquiries into two other high-profile disasters. Who was he?

The Daily Telegraph
Tuesday December 13th 1988

Air Disasters

1. The fire that destroyed the hydrogen-filled German airship *Hindenburg* on **6 May 1937**, as it came in to land in the United States, marked the end of this form of aerial transport – at least for the rest of the 20th century. The tragedy killed 36 people, including 13 passengers. How did most of the victims die?

2. The engine of a British Airtours aircraft caught fire at Manchester International Airport during take off, resulting in the deaths of 55 passengers and crew, mostly from the effects of smoke inhalation. In which year did this tragedy take place? And to which country was the aircraft heading?

3. In 1972 members of a group of rugby players involved in a plane crash in the Andes were forced to eat their dead companions in order to survive. Their story was later made into a movie. From which country did these desperate survivors come?

4. A jet aircraft with five people on board flew out of control halfway across the United States in October 1999 before crashing into a field in South Dakota. Everyone on board was thought to have become unconscious through lack of oxygen well before the plane hit the ground. Which well-known sportsman died in the crash?

5. The supersonic airliner Concorde generally had an excellent safety record in its long history but on 25 July 2000 a total of 13 people died when a jet was involved in an accident. All other Concordes were grounded as a result. From which airport had this plane just taken off when it crashed?

6. A Chinook helicopter crashed into a hillside in thick fog in June 1994, killing the crew and 25 military, police and security personnel, many of whom were senior anti-terrorist officials. On which well-known part of the British landscape did the helicopter crash?

7. Manchester United football club, and the whole of European soccer, suffered a huge tragedy in February 1958 when many of its players died in a plane crash at Munich as the squad returned to the UK. Which team had United just played and drawn against in the European Cup?

8. One of the worst aviation disasters in history occurred when in poor visibility two airliners collided on the runway of an airport on a popular holiday island. The accident in March 1977 caused the death of 583 passengers and crew. Name the island, and the two airlines whose planes were involved.

9. In October 1930 the doomed R101 airship took off from Britain and crashed hours later on a hillside near Beauvais in France; though it was only travelling at 13mph at the time, 48 people died in the disaster. One of the passengers on board was Lord (Christopher) Thomson – what was his official government position at the time? What had been the aircraft's intended destination?

10. In July 2002 a Russian-built Sukhoi Su-27 aircraft flew out of control while performing aerobatics at an air show. The two pilots ejected to safety and survived but the plane ploughed through watching spectators, killing a total of 84 people. In which country did this air disaster take place?

**The Daily Mail
Friday May 7th 1937**

Nautical Disasters

1. In March 1987 the *Herald of Free Enterprise* ferry capsized as it left the port of Zeebrugge when water flooded into its car deck. It is thought the water got into the ferry because the bow doors had been left open as it left port. The final death toll was 193. What was the verdict of the jury at the inquest into the deaths? To which port was the ferry heading?

2. The liner *Titanic* was heading for New York as it set out on its ill-fated voyage in 1912 from Southampton, from where many of its crew came. But which was the last port it visited before striking the iceberg that sank it?

3. A Greek ferry called *Express Samina* hit rocks off the island of Paros resulting in 80 deaths – though the death toll could have been even higher if local fishermen had not picked up many survivors from the water. In which year did this tragedy occur? Was it:
a 1998
b 1999
c 2000

4. During a yacht race in the Irish Sea in August 1979 a freak storm hit the competitors with disastrous results. Many yachts were lost and 15 people died, six of them because their safety harnesses broke. What was the name of the race?

5. A car and passenger ferry sunk in the Baltic Sea in bad weather in 1994 with the loss of 852 lives; the tragedy was partly blamed on the design of the ferry's front doors. What was the name of the ferry and to which country was it heading at the time?

6. December 1987 saw one of the worst sea tragedies in recent history, involving the Philippine ferry *Dona Paz* and the loss of more than 4,000 lives. What happened to the ferry?

Sunk without trace

7. Though it did not bring the United States into the First World War, the loss of many US citizens on board this ship, when it was sunk by a German submarine, caused severe tensions between the two countries. What was the name of the vessel and in which year was it torpedoed?

8. In a 1989 tragedy on the River Thames 51 people died when the pleasure cruiser *Marchioness* collided with another vessel; the victims were young party-goers who were enjoying a night out on the river boat. What was the name and type of the boat that collided with the *Marchioness*?

9. A ferry capsized off the west coast of Africa in September 2002, killing up to 1,000 people. Overloading was partly to blame for the disaster, as the ferry was designed to carry 550 people but had more than 1,000 on board when it capsized. To which country did the ferry belong? Was it:
a Senegal
b Gambia
c Liberia

10. In February 1974 a British trawler sank in the Arctic Circle north of Norway with the loss of all 36 crew on board. In 2004 an inquiry discounted theories that the trawler had been sunk by the Russians or that a British submarine became entangled in its nets. What was the trawler's name? At which port was it based?

The Mail on Sunday
March 8th 1987

Space Disasters

1. The space shuttle *Challenger* blew up soon after take off, killing all seven crew on board. The dead included Christa McAuliffe who was to be the first school teacher in space and the disaster – captured live on television – was a huge blow to the American space programme. When did the US resume manned flights? Was it:

a 1987
b 1988
c 1989

2. Space exploration has become popular with many nations around the world, but ever since the pioneering days it has been potentially hazardous and many people have died either in training or during missions. Of which nationality was the first person to die in an in-flight space mission? In which year was it?

3. Three American astronauts perished while training for the *Apollo 1* mission in 1967: Virgil Grissom, Edward White and Roger Chaffee. In what circumstances did they die?

4. The *Apollo 13* moon mission nearly turned into a major disaster when there was an explosion on board, and the dramatic story of how it got back to earth safely was later made into a popular film starring Tom Hanks as astronaut Jim Lovell. In which year did the incident take place?

5. Amid much embarrassing publicity a British space probe whose aim was to see if there is life on Mars went missing in December 2003; what was the name of the scientist in charge of the project, what was the probe's name, and after whom or what was it named?

6. In September 1999 scientists at NASA lost contact with their *Mars Climate Orbiter* space probe. It later emerged that the loss of the $125million probe was due to an embarrassing mix-up between two sets of engineers who had worked on it. What was that blunder?

7. In the early days of space exploration animals were used to test the effects of space travel on living species, and as early as 1950 a mouse had been sent into space by the US on a V2 rocket. However, the first animal to go into orbit was on board *Sputnik 2* in 1957 – though sadly it did not survive the experience. What species of animal was it and what was its name?

8. The American space shuttle programme was hit by a second major disaster when a shuttle broke up as it re-entered the earth's atmosphere after a two-week mission in 2003. All seven crew on board perished, including Israel's first astronaut, Ilan Ramon. What was the name of this shuttle?

9. In February 1996 a test rocket veered off course moments after take off, crashing into a nearby village. At least six inhabitants were killed, more than 50 injured and around 80 homes were demolished. In which country did this occur?

10. The two-man crew of the Soviet spacecraft *Voskhod 2* finally made it back to earth in 1965 after a number of mishaps and technical problems. What unexpected hazard did they have to face before they were recovered from their module?

Daily Mail
Wednesday January 29th 1986

19

Chemical and Fire Disasters

1. A fire on a North Sea platform in July 1988 left more than 160 people dead. The platform was one of the biggest and also oldest in the sea, and its safety procedures were later criticised during a top-level inquiry chaired by Lord Cullen. What was the platform called and who were its owners?

2. One of the worst chemical disasters in British history was at a chemical plant at Flixborough, near Scunthorpe, where an explosion killed 28 people. In which year did this occur? Was it
a 1966
b 1970
c 1974

3. The chemical disaster at Bhopal in India was probably the worst of its kind in history. A cloud of toxic gas escaped from a chemical plant and passed through the city causing death and serious injury; at least 2,000 died in the immediate aftermath and many others are thought to have died in subsequent years from the effects of the chemicals. What was the name of the plant's parent company? And in which year did the disaster occur?

4. A terrible fire killed 56 fans at Bradford City football ground in 1985. What achievement had the club just celebrated?

5. In 1992 a massive fire swept through Windsor Castle, taking more than 200 firemen 15 hours to put out. Around 100 rooms were damaged and the restoration work cost £37 million, 70 per cent of it paid for by Her Majesty the Queen. What is thought to have been the cause of the blaze?

Explosion

6. The 1981 house fire that killed 13 people attending a party still remains something of a mystery and still provokes controversy; all the victims were young black men and women and it has long been claimed that there was a racial element to the blaze, with evidence suggesting that it was started deliberately. In which part of London did the fire occur?

7. When fire caused by a lightning strike badly damaged York Minster in July 1984 some claimed that it was divine retribution after the ordination of a controversial cleric there three days before. Who was that cleric and to which position had he just been ordained?

8. In December 2005 fire ripped through an oil depot near Hemel Hempstead, Hertfordshire, causing massive explosions and huge damage, and sending a spectacular cloud of fumes into the sky. What was the name of the oil depot?

9. Name the Boston nightclub at which 492 people lost their lives in a horrific fire in 1942, a disaster that led to a reform of fire codes and safety standards across the country. Also, who was the movie actor – the star of many Westerns – who died in the fire?

10. A French city was rocked by a huge explosion at a factory in September 2001, which killed at least 29 people and left hundreds more injured. The blast was so massive it was said to be equivalent to a magnitude 3.2 earthquake on the Richter scale. Which city was it? What type of factory was it?

**The Daily Telegraph
Friday July 8th 1988**

The Daily Telegraph

169 dead in North Sea disaster

Gas leak blamed for explosions that split Piper Alpha in two

City that knows the cost of oil

Safety inspection two weeks ago

Royal Family – Part 1

1. Who was the British Prime Minister who dealt with the Abdication Crisis in 1936 when Edward VIII was forced to choose between the throne and his love for Mrs Wallis Simpson? Which party was he from?

2. It was deemed unthinkable that Mrs Wallis Simpson could wed Edward VIII because as the ultimate head of the Church of England the king could not marry a woman who had been divorced. In fact she had been married twice before, the first time to an American military man named Earl Winfield Spencer and, after divorcing him, to businessman Ernest Simpson, whom she married in 1928. What had been her maiden name?

3. Princess Elizabeth was famously abroad in February 1952 when her father George VI died suddenly and she immediately became Queen Elizabeth II. What was the name of the place she was staying at the time, and in which country is it?

4. Royal crises, disasters and scandals have come and gone over the decades but in one year in particular there were so many difficulties that Queen Elizabeth II was moved to describe it in a speech at the Guildhall as her *annus horribilis* – her horrible year. Which year was this? Was it:
a 1990
b 1991
c 1992

5. As well as having been a leading figure in the Olympic movement, Princess Anne is a very fine horsewoman in her own right and was good enough to be part of the United Kingdom's equestrian team at one Games. In which year and where was this?

6. Though the formal investiture of Prince Charles as the Prince of Wales took place at Caernarfon in 1969, this was not the occasion when he officially became the Prince of Wales. In which year did this take place?

7. Like his sons after him, Prince Charles had a career in the military and spent a number of years in the Royal Navy. Which ship did he end up commanding while he was in the Navy and in which year did he finally leave the service?

8. The royal version of the hit TV programme *It's a Knockout*, staged in 1987, was widely ridiculed in the press. Which member of the Royal Family stormed out of a press conference after asking waiting journalists if they had enjoyed the show – and was met with a resounding silence?

9. The continued use of the Royal Yacht *Britannia* by the Royal Family became an issue of controversy as to whether its expensive upkeep represented good value for money. In which year was it finally taken out of service?

10. When she died in 2002 the much-loved Queen Elizabeth the Queen Mother had been known by that title for 50 years, ever since the death of her husband George VI and the accession of her daughter to the throne. What was her maiden name? In which year was her death prematurely announced by the media in Australia after a 'rehearsal' of coverage of her death by a British TV company had been misinterpreted?

The Star
Thursday December 10th 1936

Royal Family – Part 2

1. The unfolding saga of Prince Charles and Princess Diana's marriage and its eventual demise gripped the world's media for many years, and it ultimately emerged that for a number of years the couple had led separate lives before they split up. But when was their separation formally announced? Was it:

a 1992

b 1993

c 1994

2. Princess Diana famously declared to a TV interviewer that 'There were three of us in this marriage, so it was a bit crowded'. Who was the TV interviewer and for which programme was he working at the time? And who was the third person to whom she was referring?

3. Within hours of the tragic death of Diana, Princess of Wales, in a car crash in Paris in August 1997, her body was flown back to Britain, accompanied by her former husband Prince Charles. To which airport was her coffin flown and which flag was draped over it?

4. In which year did Princess Anne dramatically escape an attempt to kidnap her when an armed man stopped her chauffeur-driven limousine as it made its way along Pall Mall, London? Who was in the car with her at the time?

5. A man infamously broke into Buckingham Palace and spent ten minutes talking with the Queen in her bedroom before Her Majesty was able to raise the alarm. What was his name? In which year did this breach of royal security occur? And for what offence relating to an earlier incident at Buckingham Palace was the intruder eventually charged – and acquitted?

Security? What security?

6. A friend and 'guru' to Prince Charles who had been held in a Japanese prisoner of war camp in World War Two and who was noted for making the Bushmen of the Kalahari famous, died in December 1996 at the age of 90. What was his name? And in which country had he been born?

7. In 1936 when his brother Edward VIII abdicated, the new king took the title George VI and that is how he has been known to history ever since. However, this was only the fourth of his given names – what was the new monarch's first name? What had been his official title before he unexpectedly became king?

8. In 1969 there was no annual Queen's Message broadcast on Christmas Day because Her Majesty apparently felt there would be too much of her on the television that year. What was shown instead?

9. Ronald Ferguson, father of the future Duchess of York, Sarah Ferguson, was already well known to the Royal Family before his daughter married Prince Andrew. What was the honorary position in relation to the family that he had occupied for 21 years? What was his military rank? And in which year did he die after a heart attack?

10. In 1988 Prince Charles and his skiing companions were involved in a tragedy on the slopes of their resort when an avalanche killed one of the group, Major Hugh Lindsay, and badly injured another, Mrs Patti Palmer-Tomkinson. Name the resort involved.

**Daily Mail
Thursday February 29th 1996**

Natural Disasters

1. A terrible storm that hit the east coast of England and especially Canvey Island in January 1953 caused 307 deaths with around 30,000 people having to be evacuated from their homes. Another European country was even worse hit by the storm, with more than 1,800 dying as a result. What was that country?

2. Turkey had the great misfortune to be struck by two large earthquakes in the space of just three months. The first at Izmit in the month of August left 17,000 people dead while in November, a second powerful tremor 60 miles east in the province of Bolu killed hundreds more. In which year did the quakes occur?

3. On Boxing Day 2004 a huge earthquake measuring more than 9 on the Richter scale caused a huge tsunami that left more than 280,000 people dead in Indonesia, Sri Lanka, India and Thailand and elsewhere in the Indian Ocean. On Boxing Day the year before another powerful earthquake had killed 30,000 people – in which country?

4. Tornadoes are an accepted hazard in many American states but in one year a staggering 148 tornadoes struck across 13 states, leaving 330 people dead and injuring thousands more in the space of two days. It became known as the Super Tornado Outbreak– and took place in which year? Was it:
a 1953
b 1974
c 1999

5. In September 1938 a powerful hurricane hit New England in the United States, causing massive damage and claiming up to 500 lives; one gust of wind was measured at 186mph and even the Empire State Building recorded winds of 120mph. What was the common name given to this hurricane?

6. The 1985 earthquake that devastated much of Mexico City was a huge public tragedy that left thousands of people dead and hundreds of thousands homeless. It was also a private tragedy for a famous international performer who lost four relatives in the earthquake; who was he?

7. A freak storm deposited nine inches of rain on north Devon and sent torrents of water rushing off Exmoor and down onto a coastal village. The floodwaters killed more than 30 people, left many more homeless, and swept 38 cars out to sea. What was the name of this village and in which year did this occur?

8. The infamous Great Storm of October 1987 cut a huge swathe through much of southern Britain – 18 people died and damage was estimated at £1billion, with a large number of trees uprooted. Approximately how many trees were thought to have been lost? Was it:
a one million
b eight million
c fifteen million

9. In 1983 a series of deadly fires killed 76 people and destroyed more that 2,000 homes, while more than half a million hectares were burnt and 350,000 farm animals perished. The grisly episode became known as 'Ash Wednesday'. In which country did this disaster take place?

10. One of the worst natural disasters to hit the world in recent history occurred in Tangshan, China, where an earthquake measuring at least 8 on the Richter scale left an estimated 240,000 to 650,000 dead. In which year did this take place?

The Star
Monday February 2nd 1953

Killers

1. Despite fleeing across the Atlantic on board the SS *Montrose* with his lover, the infamous killer Dr Hawley Harvey Crippen was caught by the authorities and eventually hanged in London in 1910 for the murder of his wife. What technological advance enabled him to be captured?

2. In 1989 an American was executed having confessed to 30 murders across the country, although it is claimed he may have killed as many as 100 people. His crimes helped give rise to the modern concept of a 'serial killer'. What was his name? In which State was he executed and by what means?

3. A former shopkeeper walked into a primary school in Dunblane, Scotland and fired 105 rounds of ammunition. He killed 16 young children and one teacher before committing suicide. What was this man's name? In which year did it happen?

4. The family GP Dr Harold Shipman, who killed himself in his prison cell in Wakefield Prison, was convicted of murdering 15 patients, though it has been suggested that he was responsible for many, many more. Where was he working as a GP when he was caught? In which year did he commit suicide?

5. The man known as the Yorkshire Ripper, Peter Sutcliffe, was convicted in 1981 of the murder of 13 women and attacks on several more. His arrest and eventual conviction followed a massive police hunt across northern England. What was Sutcliffe's occupation?

6. The world was shocked in 1999 when two pupils at an American high school went on the rampage, shooting fellow pupils and a teacher before finally killing themselves. What was the name of the school involved and in which US state is it?

7. The notorious Fred West killed himself in prison on 1 January 1995 before he faced trial, but he was accused of murdering twelve young women. His wife Rose was later found guilty of ten murders. The house where many of the murders occurred was later demolished; what was the name of the street and in which city was it?

8. John Christie was a British serial killer of the 1940s and 1950s who lived in Kensington, London, and who was found guilty and hanged in 1953 for his crimes. Some of his victims were buried at the house where he lived and had been the landlord, and this address subsequently became notorious. What was it?

9. The names of Ian Brady and Myra Hindley have dominated the crime headlines in Britain since they were convicted in 1966 of murdering 10-year-old Lesley Ann Downey and teenager Edward Evans. The murders were known as the 'Moors murders' after the area where four of their five victims were buried. Name the moor.

10. A lone gunman, Michael Ryan, shattered the rural peace of Hungerford, Berkshire, when he walked through the country town with a Kalashnikov automatic rifle and a pistol, shooting indiscriminately. He shot 16 people before killing himself. In what year did this take place?

**News of the World
Sunday July 31st 1910**

Assassinations & Assassination Attempts

1. The murder of Mahatma Gandhi in 1948 as he went to a prayer meeting shocked the world; the most famous living proponent of peace and non-violence had met a bloody end. What reason did the assassin and his associates later give for wanting to kill Gandhi?

2. The Queen's cousin Lord Mountbatten was blown up and killed by an IRA bomb on board his boat in Ireland, where he traditionally spent his summer holidays at the family castle in County Sligo. In which year did this murder take place? Was it:
a 1977
b 1979
c 1981

3. The murder of the black civil rights leader Martin Luther King sparked riots in up to 100 cities across the United States. James Earl Ray was convicted of the killing, but controversy persists over whether he was really responsible. In which US city did the murder take place and in which year?

4. Pope John Paul II narrowly escaped an assassination attempt when a gunman shot him at point-blank range as the pontiff was being driven in an open-top car across St Peter's Square. What was the nationality of the gunman and to whom did the Pope attribute his survival?

5. The shooting of President John F Kennedy in Dallas, Texas, on 22 November 1963 is one of the best-known and most infamous events of the 20th century. Yet JFK was not the first US President to be assassinated; how many others had been murdered in office before him and who were they?

6. India erupted in violence after the shooting of Prime Minister Indira Gandhi in New Delhi. Her successor was her own son Rajiv who, years later, was himself killed by a suicide bomber. In which years did each assassination take place?

7. When John Hinckley tried to assassinate US President Ronald Reagan in 1981 – the President was hit in the chest by a bullet ricochet – it was apparently an attempt to impress a female celebrity with whom Hinckley had become obsessed. Who was this well-known person?

8. The French president Charles de Gaulle survived a number of assassination plots by French extremists at the start of the 1960s, notably one in August 1962 that became the basis of the acclaimed Frederick Forsyth thriller *The Day of the Jackal*. What controversial policy made de Gaulle a target for these extremists?

9. The murder of Robert Kennedy in 1968 as he campaigned for the Democratic presidential nomination inevitably brought back memories of the death of his older brother JFK. In each case a lone gunman was involved, yet claims continue that there was a wider conspiracy. In which city was Robert Kennedy shot? What was the name of the gunman?

10. The death of Israeli Prime Minister Yitzhak Rabin at the hands of a militant Israeli gunman was widely seen as a blow to the peace process in the Middle East. In which year and in which city did it take place?

**The Evening News
Friday January 30th 1948**

Ireland

1. The death of 11 people in an IRA bomb blast at a Remembrance Day service at Enniskillen in Northern Ireland caused outrage around the world. Yet afterwards one man who had lost his daughter in the blast movingly declared: 'I bear no ill will, I bear no grudge'. What was the name of this man and his daughter who was killed?

2. One of the most important steps to Irish independence was the 'Easter Rising', in which Republicans staged an armed uprising and seized control of parts of Dublin. Though the rising failed and many of its leaders were executed, it was seen as a turning point in the struggle for independence. In which year did it occur? Was it:
   a 1916
   b 1917
   c 1918

3. In May 1974 a series of car bombs hit the Irish capital Dublin and the border town of Monaghan. In all 33 people were killed in the blasts, including a pregnant woman. Many years later which organisation ultimately claimed responsibility for these acts?

4. When British troops were first deployed in Northern Ireland in modern times they were initially welcomed by many in the minority Catholic community, as they were seen as preferable to officers of the Royal Ulster Constabulary who were heavily identified with the Protestant community; this 'honeymoon' period did not last long however. In what year did this deployment take place? And who was Northern Ireland's prime minister at the time?

5. In the 1980s and 1990s a small parish in countryside near Portadown in Northern Ireland became synonymous with

MURDERERS

violent clashes between Protestants and Catholics and between Protestants and the police over the route of a march. What is the name of that parish and its church?

6. On 30 January 1972, now called Bloody Sunday, 14 civilians were killed when British troops opened fire during a civil rights demonstration in Londonderry. In 1972 a report by a British judge largely exonerated the actions of the British troops but in 1998 another senior British legal figure carried out another inquiry into the affair. Name the two judges.

7. Though Ireland had effectively become an independent country by 1922 with the creation of the Irish Free State, it remained a member of the Commonwealth for a number of years. In which year did Eire formally leave the Commonwealth?

8. In 1988 two plain clothes British soldiers were dragged from their car and killed by mourners at a funeral in Belfast. That funeral was burying the dead from an incident days before when a loyalist gunman had killed three mourners at Milltown cemetery. Who was that loyalist?

9. A hunger strike by Republican prisoners over conditions at a prison in Belfast provoked headlines all around the world, especially when the British Prime Minister Margaret Thatcher made it clear she was not prepared to give way to their demands while they refused food. The first hunger striker died on 5 May 1981 – who was he? What was the name of the prison?

10. In which year did British and Irish Prime Ministers Tony Blair and Bertie Ahern plus politicians from Northern Ireland reach the so-called Good Friday peace agreement?

**The Times
Monday November 9th 1987**

Espionage

1. Anthony Blunt was a part of the Cambridge spy ring that worked for the Soviet Union during the Cold War, but he was not outed as the so-called 'Fourth Man' in the group until much later. What position did he occupy at the time, in what year was he outed – and who formally announced this in the House of Commons?

2. Along with Anthony Blunt, other known members of the Cambridge spy ring were Kim Philby, Guy Burgess and Donald MacLean. At university Blunt and Burgess were both members of a highly secretive elite debating society. What was this society known as?

3. The most dangerous and damaging of the Cambridge spy ring was Kim Philby, who occupied a senior position in the security service MI6 and kept the Russians informed of British and American security issues. Eventually Philby was unmasked as the so-called 'Third Man' in the ring. In which year did he defect to the Soviet Union?

4. One of the most famous names in espionage history is Mata Hari – real name Margaretha Zelle – an exotic dancer of Dutch extraction who was accused of spying for the Germans. In which country and in which year was she executed?

5. In 1946 an Anglo-French woman was posthumously awarded the George Cross for her extraordinary bravery as a secret agent in occupied France during the Second World War; her courage was later made famous in a book and film called *Carve her Name with Pride*. What was her name?

6. A member of the US Navy began spying for the Soviet Union in 1968 and continued for 17 years; thanks to a network of family and friends he even carried on passing over information to the Russians after he retired from the Navy and is thought to have earned up to $1 million from his espionage. What is his name?

7. To the outside world she was a little old lady of 87 who made homemade jam; but then it was revealed that Melita Norwood had been a Soviet spy for four decades, passing on nuclear information to the USSR through her work as secretary to the Non-Ferrous Metals Research Association. In which year was she exposed? Was it:

a 1995
b 1997
c 1999

8. In 1985 the defection of Hans-Joachim Tiedge from West Germany to East Germany caused a stir not just nationally but internationally too. What position had he held in West Germany that made his defection such a big story?

9. Retired Leeds University professor Vic Allen said in 1999 that he had no regrets about passing information to a foreign country's security services during the Cold War. To which security service had he passed the information and for which pressure group had he been a prominent member?

10. Amid great controversy, a husband and wife were executed in the United States after they were convicted of being part of a conspiracy to pass secrets to the Soviet Union. What were their names and in which year were they put to death?

**Daily Mail
Wednesday November 21st 1979**

Labour Disputes

1. The General Strike of May 1926 saw up to two million British workers withdraw their labour. The government led by Prime Minister Stanley Baldwin had to call on troops and volunteers to maintain food supplies and essential services. On behalf of which group of workers was the strike called? How many days did the General Strike last?

2. The Jarrow March was a famous protest march made by 200 men from the north-east of England to London in an attempt to get work for people at a time of great poverty and unemployment in much of the country. In which year did this march take place? Was it:
a 1936
b 1937
c 1938

3. A strike lasting 232 days from August 1984 affected a well-known sport in the United States in a dispute over salary structures and levels. The strike badly dented the sport's popularity even when it was over. Which sport was it?

4. A year-long strike involving print unions over the relocation of a newspaper group to a new printing plant at Wapping, east London and the imposition of new working terms was one of the most bitter in recent decades in the United Kingdom. In which year did it start? And what was the name of the newspaper publishers?

5. The period from late 1978 to early 1979 became popularly known as the 'Winter of Discontent', with growing industrial unrest and strikes affecting Britain. A strike by which small but newsworthy group of workers in Liverpool and Tameside caused some ghoulish headlines during this period?

It's All Out!

6. One of the most high-profile labour disputes in the 1970s was at a film processing plant in north London. The dispute – which involved a fight for union recognition – lasted nearly two years and involved violent clashes outside the plant. What was the factory called?

7. The oil crisis of 1973, a three-day week and looming industrial unrest from miners were the backdrop to Conservative Prime Minister Ted Heath's decision to call a snap election in 1974. In which month did the election take place and who became prime minister of a minority government as a result?

8. The miners' strike that began in 1984 was one of the most divisive and damaging labour disputes in British history. Scenes of violence involving police and miners shocked the nation. Some of the worst scenes were witnessed at a coking plant near Sheffield on 29 May 1984. What was the name of the plant? In which month and year did the strike end?

9. One of the most widespread general strikes in recent world history took place in France where after initial student strikes some ten million workers – about two-thirds of the workforce – took part in action that brought the country to its knees. In which year did these strikes take place?

10. In a memorable speech at the 1985 party conference Labour leader Neil Kinnock attacked what he called the 'grotesque' spectacle of a council's left-wing leadership 'hiring taxis to scuttle round a city handing out redundancy notices to its own workers'. Which was the city council concerned and who was its flamboyant and high-profile deputy leader?

The British Worker
Wednesday May 5th 1926

World War One

1. The mud of Flanders, where opposing troops fought each other in the most appalling conditions, became one of the great and terrible symbols of the fighting in World War One. What was the name of the Belgian town in Flanders that gave its name to three major battles?

2. Britain declared itself at war in August 1914 after the Government failed to obtain German assurances about respecting the neutrality of Belgium. Who was the British prime minister at the start of the war and which party was he from? Who succeeded him in 1916?

3. Though the war is known for its almost unrelenting death and destruction, there were occasions when the opposing sides fraternised with each other. One such time was the famous Christmas Truce when British, German and other troops met in No Man's Land; some even played football together. In which year did this take place? Was it:

a 1914
b 1915
c 1916

4. The Battle of the Somme was an attack by British and French troops against German lines and is perhaps the battle that best sums up the tactics and the massive slaughter that took place in this war. The British Expeditionary Force alone suffered nearly 60,000 casualties on the first day of the offensive, a third of them fatal. Which general was in charge of this British attack?

5. Events in the First World War were not focused entirely on the Western Front. In March 1917 British and Indian troops occupied which major Middle Eastern city? Who had been the rulers of the city till this point?

6. On 31 May 1915 the Germans carried out a bombing raid against London that killed seven people and injured more than 30 others. Which type of aircraft carried out this attack?

7. The doomed attempt to gain control of the Gallipoli peninsula in 1915 cost the lives of thousands of Allied servicemen, many of them young recruits from Australia and New Zealand. The aim had been to gain control of which strategically important stretch of water?

8. Though fighting in the First World War is mostly associated with the terrible battles on land, there was also significant activity at sea. The biggest naval battle of the war – in which 25 ships were sunk with a great loss of life – took place in May 1916. What was the battle called?

9. Aerial warfare developed in the First World War and many of the fighter pilots who flew above the trenches acquired hero status in France, Britain and Germany. Who was Germany's most successful and famous air ace, what was his nickname and in which year did he die?

10. The end of the fighting occurred at 11am on 11 November 1918 with the signing of the Armistice, but the formal document outlining the terms of peace between the warring countries was not signed until June 1919. The harsh terms of this treaty are often blamed for helping to cause World War Two; what was it called?

The Daily Mirror
Thursday September 6th 1917

Hitler

1. Though he became dictator of Germany, and utterly transformed that country's history in the middle of the 20th century, Hitler was famously not born in Germany itself. Where was he born and in what year?

2. As a young man Hitler moved to live in Munich in Bavaria, and when the First World War broke out he joined a Bavarian regiment, even though he had previously been described as unfit for military duty. Which rank did he reach in the army?

3. Hitler tried to seize power in Germany as early as 1923 when he and his supporters staged a rebellion in Munich, though the attempt quickly ended in failure and earned him a jail sentence. Hitler was also injured in the aftermath of the attempt. By what name is that failed coup commonly known?

4. From the beginning Hitler's attempts at politics went hand in hand with the use of force, and his new National Socialist or Nazi party had a paramilitary section that was important in his rise to power. The group was officially known as the *Sturmabteilung* or SA. What was its nickname? The group was purged by Hitler in 1934 – by what popular name was this event known?

5. The burning down of the German parliament building, the Reichstag, in Berlin was an important moment in Hitler's rise to ultimate power in Germany. Though no one is sure who started the fire, Hitler used it as an excuse to extend his grip on the country and clamp down on enemies. In which year did it occur? Was it;
a 1931
b 1932
c 1933

DICTATOR

6. The first part of Hitler's autobiographical and political writings, in which he displayed his bitter hatred of communism and above all Jews, was published in 1925. Ultimately up to 10 million copies of this work were sold or distributed in Germany. What were its German name and its usual English translation?

7. Hitler remained single until the final hours of his life when he married his companion of many years. What was her name and for which prominent German photographer and friend of Hitler did she work when they met?

8. During the Second World War Hitler often stayed at a military HQ at a place near Rastenburg in East Prussia (now Ketrzyn in Poland). This secret HQ had a code name – what is it in English?

9. In 1944 many senior figures in the German military were involved in a plot to assassinate Hitler with a bomb. Though the bomb exploded and killed a number of people, the Führer himself was protected from the blast by a table and escaped with minor injuries. By what name is the plot often known?

10. Shortly before his death in his Berlin bunker in April 1945 Hitler gave orders that his body should be burnt afterwards so it could not be paraded in public by his conquerors. His order was carried out and his corpse was doused with petrol and set alight. But how had he died?

**The Daily Mirror
Monday September 4th 1939**

Appeasement

1. The politician most associated with the widely-criticised policy of 'appeasement' of the fascist powers in Europe was British Prime Minister Neville Chamberlain, even though he was not alone in adopting this course of action. In which year did he become premier, and in which year did he die?

2. After the signing of the Munich Agreement in September 1938 Chamberlain flew back to Britain and later spoke in Downing Street about the outcome of the agreement. The historic headlines associated with his remarks usually refer to the line 'Peace in our time'; but what words did he actually use?

3. Also in September 1938, Chamberlain gave a radio broadcast in which he said: 'How horrible, fantastic, incredible it is that we should be digging trenches and trying on gas-masks here because of a quarrel in a far-away country between people of whom we know nothing!' The country in question was Czechoslovakia but which part of that country was the subject of the agreement between Britain and Germany at Munich?

4. Though the Munich Agreement was popular in much of Britain because it was felt it had averted a major war, not all politicians agreed with the policy of appeasement. In February 1938 the Foreign Secretary had resigned over the issue. What was the name of the man who resigned and who replaced him in the post?

5. Apart from Chamberlain, other signatories of the Munich Agreement included Adolf Hitler, Benito Mussolini and the French premier Edouard Daladier. Czechoslovakia's head of state, however, was not invited to attend the meeting. What was his name?

6. The annexation of Austria by Hitler's regime in Germany had been expressly forbidden by the terms of the Treaty of Versailles. By which German word was this annexation or 'union' best known? And in which month and year did it occur?

7. One of the main fears of the British public in the 1930s was that another war would result in widespread and unstoppable aerial bombing. In 1932 one politician declared: 'I think it is well for the man on the street to realise that there is no power on earth that can protect him from being bombed . . . the bomber will always get through.' Who was he?

8. Since the end of the First World War there had been an international organisation whose job it was to resolve conflicts and disputes, though it failed to produce any peaceful outcome to the increasingly explosive situation in Europe in the 1930s. What was its name?

9. When the German Army defied the terms of the Munich Agreement and occupied the whole of Czechoslovakia, it became clear to everyone that the policy of appeasement had not succeeded in satisfying Hitler's territorial ambitions. In which month and year did this take place?

10. Chamberlain remained as prime minister until after the outbreak of war in September 1939. He finally resigned in May 1940, a few days after Conservative politician Leo Amery had famously told him during a Parliamentary debate: 'In the name of God, go.' From which historical figure was Amery quoting?

Daily Sketch
Saturday October 1st 1938

World War Two – Part 1

1. Though the war officially began on 3 September 1939 when Germany invaded Poland, much of Western Europe remained largely untouched by fighting until Hitler's occupation of Denmark and Norway in the spring of 1940 followed by the invasion of Holland, Belgium and then France. By what name is the period between September 1939 and spring 1940 usually known?

2. At the start of the Second World War there was a non-aggression pact between the Soviet Union and Germany, though this did not prohibit Russia from invading a European neighbour on 30 November 1939. Which country was it?

3. The retreat from France in May and June 1940 – carried out with the help of the Royal Navy and a flotilla of private craft – is one of the most famous events in British military history. What was the name of the group that had been sent to France to fight the Nazis and whose soldiers had to be evacuated at Dunkirk?

4. The Battle of Britain, the bitter combat between the RAF and the German Luftwaffe in 1940, was one of the most important battles in the early part of the Second World War. In which month did it start and in which month did it officially end?

5. A key outcome of the Battle of Britain was that the RAF's victory postponed indefinitely Hitler's plans for an invasion of Britain, an event that most people in the country had feared was imminent. What was the code name for this planned invasion?

6. After deciding against invading Britain, Hitler turned his gaze eastwards and despite his pact with Russia launched a massive assault on the Soviet Union. In which month and year did this start, and what was its codename?

Bombed Out

7. The surprise Japanese bombing of the base at Pearl Harbor shocked the American people and brought the United States into World War Two. On which Hawaiian island is Pearl Harbor? In which month and year did the attack happen?

8. The fall of Singapore to the Japanese in February 1942 was a devastating blow to the British war effort and morale. Two months earlier the Japanese had sunk two British warships whose task it was to defend Singapore, an event that led Prime Minister Winston Churchill to say later: 'In all the war I never received a more direct shock.' Name one of the two ships.

9. The fascist leader Benito Mussolini wanted to emulate Hitler's military triumphs early in the war and in October 1940 the Italians launched an invasion of their own, though in the end it ended in failure. Which country did they attack?

10. In October 1940 the Spanish dictator General Franco met Adolf Hitler to discuss the possible involvement of neutral Spain in the war; though in the end Spain stayed on the sidelines despite its sympathies for Nazi Germany and Fascist Italy. In which town and country did they meet?

**Evening Standard
Friday May 10th 1940**

World War Two – Part 2

1. In August 1944 Allied troops – symbolically led by a French armoured division – liberated Paris from Nazi rule. Despite sporadic fighting the city was taken intact and largely undamaged and the leader of the Free French, General Charles de Gaulle, was able to lead a procession down the Champs-Elysées. What had been Hitler's orders to the German troops defending the city?

2. The long awaited D-Day landings on 6 June 1944 in Normandy marked the beginning of the end for German occupation of much of Western Europe, and involved troops from twelve countries including the United States, Britain, Canada, France, Australia and Poland. Who was the general in overall command of the invasion and what was its codename?

3. The desert battle of El Alamein in 1942, which was won decisively by the British, is often seen as a significant moment in the development of the war. What was the name of the German commander involved, what was his nickname and what was the name of the army he commanded?

4. In January 1946 the broadcaster who became known as Lord Haw Haw, and who during the war had made regular radio broadcasts from Germany, in English, that urged the British people to surrender, was hanged for treason. What was his real name?

5. The French Resistance played an important role during the war, uniting local opposition to German occupation, helping Allied troops and harassing German troops in the build-up to the invasion of France. A nickname of this mainly rural resistance was taken from the geography of some of the areas they fought in; what was it?

Victory At Last!

6. By February 1943 Soviet forces – at huge cost to themselves – had successfully repulsed a determined siege of an important city and in doing so wiped out an entire German army, whose soldiers were either killed or taken prisoner. Which city had the Germans besieged? And which army did they lose?

7. After their execution in April 1945 at the hands of Italian partisans the bodies of the Italian dictator Benito Mussolini and his mistress Claretta Petacci, were hung upside down from a lamp post. In which city did this grisly occurrence take place? Was it:
a Rome
b Venice
c Milan

8. The Soviet Marshall who was largely instrumental in the fall of Berlin in 1945 had also helped organise the counter-attack by the Russians at Stalingrad. What was his name? And who was the German commander who took over as the German head of state after Hitler's suicide?

9. The dropping of the world's first atomic bomb on Hiroshima on 6 August 1945 hastened the end of the war, though it took a second bomb on Nagasaki and a Soviet declaration of war against Japan before the Japanese finally surrendered. What was the name of the plane that dropped that first bomb?

10. At the conference held at Potsdam, Germany, in the summer of 1945 to discuss how Germany should be ruled and to issue a surrender ultimatum to Japan, the Soviet Union was represented by its leader Joseph Stalin. Which leaders represented the United States and the United Kingdom respectively?

Sunday Pictorial
August 27th 1944

Churchill

1. The death of Sir Winston Churchill in January 1965 was headline news all around the world, and he was the first statesman in the twentieth century to be given a state funeral in Britain. Where did the funeral service take place, and how did London dockers pay their respects as his funeral barge went along the Thames?

2. Winston Spencer Churchill came from a well-known English family and had some colourful and influential forebears. In particular one of his ancestors of the late seventeenth/early eighteenth century was considered one of the ablest military commanders the country had ever produced. Who was he?

3. As a young man Churchill embarked on a brief military career. However, when he was captured during a war – though he subsequently escaped – he was not employed as a soldier at the time. What was his occupation, and in which conflict did this take place?

4. Churchill was interested in politics from an early age though he did not always remain loyal to one party throughout his long career. For which political party did he win the Manchester North West seat in the 1906 General Election?

5. One of the many controversies in Churchill's life was his involvement in the ill-fated Allied landings at Gallipoli in 1915 during the First World War. What was Churchill's position at the start of the war, and what rather more dangerous posting did he volunteer for after resigning from the government in 1916?

6. Churchill married in 1908 and away from the glare and controversy of his public life enjoyed a relatively stable family life. What was the name of the woman he married and what was the name of the house in Kent in which they lived from 1922?

7. Though Churchill is best known for his roles in wartime governments, he also served as a Cabinet minister between the wars, notably when he became Chancellor of the Exchequer in 1924. However in that job he promoted a policy that proved harmful for Britain's economy, and which he later described as one of the worst decisions of his life. What was that policy?

8. During his so-called wilderness years of the 1930s Churchill was one of the few leading figures to warn about the prospects of impending war in Europe and the dangers of the rise of fascism in Germany. What job was he given after war finally broke out in September 1939?

9. One of the great qualities Churchill showed during his leadership in World War Two was his ability to sum up situations with memorable and inspiring speeches. On one occasion he referred to an event as being 'not the end . . . It is not even the beginning of the end. But it is, perhaps, the end of the beginning.' To which event was he referring?

10. Alongside his political career Churchill was a prolific historian and writer and he produced popular works such as the *History of the English-Speaking Peoples*. However it was as much for his oratorical prowess that Churchill was given which prestigious award in 1953?

The Times
Monday January 25th 1965

International Crises/ Cold War – Part 1

1. The Suez Crisis of 1956 deeply strained relations between Britain and the United States – who opposed military intervention – and led to the resignation of the British Prime Minister Sir Anthony Eden. Which action by President Nasser of Egypt provoked Israeli, British and French military involvement in the area?

2. One of the most dramatic events in the Cold War was the 'Berlin Airlift' in which Allied planes flew in supplies for the inhabitants of Western-controlled parts of Berlin after the Soviet Union blockaded the city. The airlift lasted for more than 300 days. In which year did it start?

3. The Cuban missile crisis brought the world close to nuclear war, when the Americans opposed Soviet plans to install rockets on Cuba, near the US mainland. Who were the respective Soviet and American leaders at the time and in which year did it occur?

4. After the Second World War the French tried to re-impose their influence in Vietnam until a decisive military defeat at the hands of the Vietminh in May 1954 persuaded the authorities in Paris to withdraw from the region. What was the name of this famous battle?

5. The Tet Offensive launched by the National Liberation Army is often described as a major turning point in the Vietnam War. Though it resulted in a military defeat for the NLF, it showed they still had the resources to mount large-scale attacks despite the presence of so many US troops. In which year did it occur? Was it:

    a 1968
    b 1971
    c 1974

6. The Rwandan Genocide of 1994 left around 800,000 people dead and highlighted the failure of the international community in general and the United Nations in particular to maintain peace and stability in the country. Who were the two ethnic groups involved in this awful tragedy?

7. Tensions between India and Pakistan have periodically resulted in violent clashes ever since the countries were divided and became independent in the process known as partition in 1947; one of the most serious occasions was in 1971 when full-scale war broke out. Which country gained independence as a result of this crisis and what was its former name?

8. In the long and often bloody conflict in Bosnia, one of the worst atrocities took place at Srebrenica, where thousands of Muslims were massacred by Bosnian Serbs. What official UN status did Srebrenica have at the time of the slaughter? In which year did this massacre occur?

9. The Democratic Republic of Congo – formerly Zaire – became involved in an international crisis almost as soon as it became independent, involving the deployment of thousands of UN troops. From which country did it win independence and in which year?

10. One of the most famous headlines in British tabloid newspaper history – 'Gotcha' – came during the Falklands War in 1981. The headline referred to the attack on an Argentine ship. What was the name of the Argentine ship and the name and type of the British craft that sunk it?

**Daily Sketch
Wednesday October 31st 1956**

International Crises/ Cold War – Part 2

1. The Korean War was one of the first major conflicts of the Cold War and involved troops from China and the United States, as well as Soviet weaponry and UN troops. In which year did this war officially end?

2. Though he is now dead, the man who became leader of North Korea after its independence in 1948 is still officially known in the country's constitution as its 'eternal president' as well as its 'Great Leader'. What was his name, in which year did he die and who succeeded him?

3. In 1960 the Soviet Union shot down an American U2 spy plane, an episode that heightened tensions between the US and Russia. The pilot, who survived, was later given a ten-year prison sentence though he was soon exchanged for a Soviet spy. What was the pilot called?

4. The war that eventually resulted in Algerian independence in 1962 was a bitter and bloody affair that affected not just events in North Africa but in France too. One complication was the presence in Algeria of a large minority of European-descended residents, a vast number of whom fled the country in 1962. By what name are they still popularly known?

5. The massacre of hundreds – perhaps thousands – of students by Chinese troops in Beijing's huge Tiananmen Square caused international outrage. One powerful photographic image of those events dominated media coverage – what did it depict? In which year did the massacre occur?

Iron Curtain

6. The highly-publicised conflict known as the Biafran War caused a massive loss of life in the late 1960s, with many of the victims falling prey to disease and starvation rather than the fighting. The conflict was essentially a civil war; in which African country did it take place?

7. The costly war between Iran and Iraq that ended in 1988 may have resulted in the deaths of as many as one million people, and it certainly caused billions of pounds' worth of damage. In which year did this bitter conflict start?

8. When Pol Pot seized power in Cambodia in 1975 he instituted a reign of genocidal terror and extreme economic policy that led to the deaths of up to a million people. What was the name of his infamous organisation and to what did the country change its name in 1975?

9. The famine that gripped drought-stricken Ethiopia in the mid-Eighties cost around one millions lives. Rock star Bob Geldof came to prominence for his role in organising the Live Aid rock concerts, but who was the TV newsman whose powerful stories on the plight of Ethiopians helped bring the tragedy into Britons' homes?

10. The fall of the Berlin Wall in 1989 marked the effective end of the Cold War and led to the re-unification of Germany. In which year had construction of the wall started, and what is the name of the place that marked the meeting point between East and West Berlin? And what was the name of the long-serving East German leader who was deposed just before the wall fell?

Daily Graphic
Wednesday June 28th 1950

Landmark British Political Events – Part 1

1. Despite his inspiring leadership of the country during the Second World War Sir Winston Churchill and his party were convincingly defeated in the 1945 General Election by Labour, who won a landslide majority of 159 seats. Who became the new prime minister and for how many years did Labour then stay in power?

2. The most notable step taken by the 1945 Labour government was the development of the welfare state in Britain. It was based largely on a report that had been written in 1942 and that had recommended a national health service and a social insurance system to protect people 'from the cradle to the grave'. What was the name of that report?

3. In the early part of the twentieth century a new Parliament Act came into force that significantly curtailed the power of the House of Lords to block or delay legislation put forward by the democratically-elected government of the day. In which year was the Act passed and who was prime minister at the time?

4. One of most powerful figures of twentieth-century British politics was David Lloyd George, a reforming Chancellor of the Exchequer and the last Liberal leader to be prime minister of the United Kingdom. In which year did he leave office as prime minister?

5. After the demise of Lloyd George the Liberal Party was replaced by the emerging Labour Party as the main opposition to the Conservatives. In which year did the first Labour administration take office, and who was the first Labour prime minister?

Landslide!

6. Labour Prime Minister Harold Wilson sought to reassure the British public that a decision just taken by his government would not affect the 'pound in your pocket'. To which decision was he referring and which year did this occur?

7. The so-called Night of the Long Knives in British politics refers to the occasion when, with the government's unpopularity growing, a British prime minister sacked no fewer than six members of the Cabinet. Who was the prime minister and in which year did this happen?

8. The speech given by the politician Enoch Powell in 1968 in which he warned of the dangers of immigration became known as the 'Rivers of blood' speech. In which city did Powell deliver this infamous speech, and which political post did he lose as a result of it?

9. Having been rebuffed twice by French president Charles de Gaulle, Britain finally joined the European Economic Community (EEC) in 1973. Two other nations also joined, bringing the number of members to nine. Who were those two countries? And who were the six existing members?

10. The resignation of Harold Wilson as prime minister in 1976 came as a shock to the nation; he was only 60 at the time. Sir Harold as he then became stayed on as an MP until finally taking a peerage. What title did he take as a peer – and who succeeded him as Labour leader and prime minister?

Evening Standard
Thursday July 26th 1945

Landmark British Political Events – Part 2

1. A year before Margaret Thatcher quit as prime minister she easily fought off a challenge from a so-called 'stalking horse' candidate. However, on 1 November 1990 a senior Cabinet member resigned, and later gave a powerful speech in the Commons that many regard as key in triggering an ultimately successful leadership campaign. Who was the 'stalking horse' and who was the senior minister?

2. Long before she became prime minister Margaret Thatcher had become a headline-grabbing figure in the 1970s when as Education Secretary she announced a controversial cutback. What was her policy and what newspaper nickname did it earn her?

3. At one general election Labour politician Gerald Kaufman famously referred to his party's manifesto as the 'the longest suicide note in history'. To which election was Kaufman referring? Was it:
a 1987
b 1979
c 1983

4. In January 1981 the so-called 'gang of four' – four prominent members of the Labour Party – held a press conference in which they revealed plans for a new council of social democracy and called for a realignment of British politics. What did this declaration become known as, and who were the four?

5. When the Liberal Party and Social Democratic Party merged to form a new party it was originally called the Social and Liberal Democrat Party, though this later became the Liberal Democrats. In which year did this merger take place and who was subsequently elected its new leader?

6. Many people thought the Labour Party might win the 1992 General Election. In fact *The Sun*, which was vehemently against a Labour victory, published the memorable headline, 'If Kinnock Wins Today Will The Last Person in Britain Please Turn Out The Light'. Some observers blamed Labour's narrow loss on an allegedly triumphal attitude it had shown at a major rally a week before polling. Where was the rally?

7. After the tragic death of Labour leader John Smith from a heart attack in May 1994, who took over as interim leader until party elections could be held?

8. There is much speculation and controversy over a so-called pact between Tony Blair and Gordon Brown, in which the latter supposedly agreed to support the former in the 1994 Labour leadership election. In return Blair was said to have agreed to step down after two terms as prime minister to make way for Brown. What was the name of the restaurant where this alleged pact was made, and in which part of London is it?

9. Elections to the Scottish Parliament and Welsh Assembly were held in 1999, after voters in each country had voted for a form of devolution in 1997. However, in referendums years earlier the Welsh people had rejected devolution while an insufficient number of Scots had voted for a devolved parliament to make it happen there. In which year did both these votes take place?

10. Leo Blair became the first child to be born to a serving British prime minister for more than 150 years. In which year was he born and who was he named after?

**Evening Standard
Thursday November 22nd 1990**

Sporting Achievements

1. England's famous win in the 1966 World Cup football finals over West Germany was not without controversy. Geoff Hurst scored his second goal to put England 3–2 up after a linesman ruled that the striker's shot had crossed the line. Hurst later completed his hat trick to make it 4–2. From which country was the linesman?

2. When football's European Cup began in the 1950s it was completely dominated by Real Madrid. In 1960 the Spanish club demolished Eintracht Frankfurt 7–3 in an extraordinary final; at which neutral venue was this match played? How many times had Real now won the competiton?

3. The greatest batsman in the history of cricket was undoubtedly the Australian Don Bradman. When he walked to the crease for his final Test innings in 1948 he needed just four runs to guarantee the incredible Test match batting average of 100. Where was this Test match held, how many runs did Bradman score – and who dismissed him?

4. The great Swedish tennis player Bjorn Borg won five consecutive Wimbledon titles and six other major titles. In which year did Borg with his fifth and last Wimbledon, whom did he beat in the final – and which major grand slam tournament did he never win despite reaching four finals?

5. The American amateur golfer Bobby Jones is arguably the best player ever to have played the sport, winning all four major golf titles in the same year – the US and British Opens, and the US and British amateur titles. In which year did Jones achieve this 'grand slam'? Was it:
a 1930
b 1931
c 1932

6. In 1958 he retired from racing after being Formula One champion five times and having won an astonishing 24 Grand Prix races out of the 51 he had started; he was also briefly kidnapped by Cuban rebels in the year he retired. Who was he and what was his nationality?

7. The celebrated horse Red Rum was bred to be a sprinter but turned into one of the best and most-loved steeplechasers in racing history. He won the Grand National at Aintree an astonishing three times, and in more than 100 outings fell just once. In which year did he die and who was his celebrated trainer?

8. The Scottish football team Celtic became not just the first British team but the first North European side to win the European Cup, an event that had hitherto been dominated by clubs from Spain, Italy and Portugal. In which year did they win the cup, who did they beat and in which country was the final held?

9. England famously won the 2003 World Cup rugby final – becoming the first Northern hemisphere team to win the competition – with a late drop goal against Australia from their fly half Jonny Wilkinson. What was the final score, and who had England beaten in the semi-final?

10. The England cricket team's memorable series victory over Australia in 2005 was the first time they had won the Ashes since 1987. Who was top of the England bowling averages and of the batting averages in the series?

**Evening Standard
Monday August 1st 1966**

59

Sporting Controversies

1. The so-called Bodyline cricket series between England and Australia in 1932/33 was dominated by the England captain Douglas Jardine's controversial policy of using his fast bowlers to bowl fast and short at the Australian batsmen – a tactic Jardine called 'Fast Leg Theory'. Who were Jardine's two principal fast bowlers and who won the series?

2. In 1999 four people were convicted in relation to a plot by a Far East betting syndicate to cut the floodlights during a football match. At which club's ground was the plot discovered in February 1999?

3. At Newton Abbot an unfancied horse called In the Money apparently won the Hatherleigh Selling Handicap Hurdles at the very decent odds of 8–1. However it later turned out the winning horse was not the unknown In the Money – but instead was Cobbler's March, a horse that had already won five races. In which year did this occur?

4. One of the earliest football scandals of the twentieth century involved Leeds City who were disbanded in 1919 after they were found guilty of having made illegal payments to players. Another club took over Leeds' fixtures for the rest of the season – who were they?

5. Australian cricket captain Greg Chappell provoked outrage in the sport in 1981 when he instructed his brother to bowl the final ball of the match delivery underarm and along the ground to ensure the other team could not hit the six they needed to win. What was Greg Chappell's brother called and who were the Australians playing?

CHEAT

6. In 1965 three footballers, Tony Kay, Peter Swann and David Layne, were convicted of conspiracy to fix matches. The high-profile players – Kay and Swann were England internationals – had been betting against their own team. Which club did they play for at the time?

7. The 1974 Lions rugby tour of South Africa was marred by on-field violence. The Lions in fact devised an infamous call which when uttered meant that all players were expected to join in a fight against the opposition. What was the call, and who was the captain of the Lions?

8. The famous Bosman ruling made by the European Court of Justice in 1995 meant that once a player's contract had ended with a football club, he was regarded as a free agent and entitled to a free transfer to another club. It also removed any quotas for clubs on foreign players as long as they came from the European Union. What was the full name of the player at the centre of the row, and which club had he been trying to leave?

9. The late South African cricket captain, Hanse Cronje, shocked his countrymen when he admitted he had taken money in return for giving 'information' to bookmakers and asking team-mates to play badly. In which year did he make this admission? And officials from which country first revealed his involvement in the scandal?

10. A German referee was convicted and jailed in 2005 after admitting fixing or trying to fix nine football matches in which he was involved. What was his name?

**Evening Standard
Monday May 22nd 1933**

Social Protests and Unrest

1. The start of the twentieth century saw many public protests supporting the right of women to vote. Perhaps the best known and most tragic was when a suffragette threw herself under the king's horse during the Derby, and later died. What was her name, what year did this happen – and in what year were women first given the right to vote?

2. The first march organised by the Campaign for Nuclear Disarmament (CND) from London to the UK's Atomic Weapons Establishment in Berkshire took place in 1958. What was the name of the centre, a name by which these annual protest marches became known?

3. The Brixton riots of April 1981 were described in a report as the worst outbreak of social disorder in the UK yet in the twentieth century. Which senior figure carried out the official inquiry into the riots? And in which part of Liverpool were there also riots that same year?

4. Opposition to the introduction of the poll tax in Britain included rioting and social disorder in London that is sometimes referred to as the Battle of Trafalgar Square. In which year did this disturbance occur, in which year did the government announce they were to abolish the poll tax – and what was its official name?

5. At Whitsun in 1964 a number of seaside resorts in southern England became the battleground for fights between rival groups of youths; in Brighton up to 1,000 youths were involved in running battles. By what names were the rival groups known?

6. In 2004 Prime Minister Tony Blair was in the chamber of the House of Commons when protestors hurled purple flour from the visitors' gallery in what was seen as a major security breach. The people who carried out the stunt were members of which protest group?

7. The Los Angeles riots of the 1990s that left more than 50 people dead were sparked by a number of factors, among them the level of unemployment and the attitude of the Los Angeles Police Department towards many blacks and Latinos. However the immediate cause was the acquittal of four police officers who had been videotaped beating a black motorist. What was the motorist's name and in what year were the riots?

8. A huge demonstration popularly known as the Countryside March brought up to 400,000 people to the streets of London in September 2002, protesting not just about a proposed ban on hunting with dogs but concerning a wide range of rural grievances. What was the official name of the protest?

9. In August 1998 some animal welfare groups condemned animal rights activists for releasing around 6,000 captive animals into the wild. What was the breed of animal they freed and in which well-known natural area were they released?

10. The *Rainbow Warrior* boat used by environmental protest organisation Greenpeace was sunk by the French secret service in July 1985, resulting in the death of one person. In which harbour was the boat at the time, and who was the French prime minister who later publicly admitted that French agents were responsible?

**The Daily Mirror
Friday April 27th 1906**

Television – History and Programmes

1. The first regular TV service in Britain came from the BBC and was launched in 1936, though few people had sets to watch it at the time. From which London landmark did the BBC begin those broadcasts?

2. The BBC's general manger in its early days was a powerful personality who took the organisation away from its commercial roots and saw its future as an independent provider of information, education and culture, free from political control – even though he did not value TV as much as radio. What was his name – and what did the letters BBC originally stand for?

3. Since the birth of television, sporting events have been an important part of the schedules. In which (same) year did the BBC first televise the annual Boat Race between Oxford and Cambridge, the FA Cup Final and also a cricket Test at Lord's?

4. After nearly two decades of monopoly, the BBC finally faced competition when commercial television in the form of ITV was launched in 1955. What was the product featured in the UK's first TV advert? And which well-known BBC radio show ran a dramatic storyline to coincide with the launch – though the BBC denied it was intended as a spoiler?

5. In July 1962 the first ever live television pictures were beamed across the Atlantic, and leading personalities Raymond Baxter and Richard Dimbleby presided over a special BBC programme to mark the achievement. What was the name of the satellite that made this possible?

Breaking News   Breaking News   Breaking News   Breaking News

6. For British television viewers the world was a black and white affair until the advent of colour TV, which then quickly became a big hit with viewers. In which year was colour television first broadcast regularly in Britain, which station was the first to use it, and who was in charge of that station and the introduction of colour TV?

7. The year 1976 was the end of an era for British television as it saw the demise of the long-running series *Dixon of Dock Green*. In which year did the series start? Was it:

a 1951
b 1953
c 1955

8. After the birth of ITV in the 1950s, the British public had to wait until 1982 for another commercial television channel to be launched. Channel Four then helped to change the face of British broadcasting with some innovative programmes. Who was its first chief executive?

9. The popular ITV soap *Coronation Street* was originally envisaged as having just a six-week run when it was launched in 1960, but it is still going strong today. Which British poet defended the programme in its early days, comparing it to Charles Dickens' *Pickwick Papers*? And who created the series?

10. Though it is now a regular part of viewers' lives, breakfast television is a relatively recent phenomenon in Britain, and was only launched in 1983. What was the name of the commercial station that began breakfast broadcasting in February of that year, and what was the name of the furry puppet credited with saving its ratings?

**Daily Sketch
Tuesday November 3rd 1936**

Celebrities & Popular Culture – Part 1

1. Elvis Presley died on 16 August 1977, aged just 42. Found lying unconscious by his road manager, Jerry Esposito, Presley was rushed to hospital but never regained consciousness. A three-hour post-mortem examination declared the cause of his death to be what? And where had Presley been found?

2. Michael Jackson was one of the most successful pop stars of the twentieth century, with 29 solo number one hits around the world. He also recorded and co-produced the album that was the best-selling album of the century. What is its name and in which year was it released?

3. On 3 February 1959, a light passenger plane crashed between Clear Lake, Iowa and Fargo, North Dakota, killing the pilot and its three rock 'n' roll passengers, Buddy Holly, Ritchie Valens and JP 'Big Bopper' Richardson. Which song by Don McLean contains references to this accident, including the line 'the day the music died...'? And in which year did it become a number one hit in the US?

4. The singer Madonna, often known as 'The Queen of Pop' has sold more than 200 million records worldwide in a career that has lasted for more than 20 years. What was her birth name and in which American city was she brought up? And which Briton did she marry in 2000?

5. One member of The Beatles famously commented in a newspaper interview that the band was 'more popular than Jesus'. Despite the Archbishop of Boston admitting that this was probably right, the words sparked outrage across America where Beatles records were destroyed and effigies burned. Which Beatle uttered those words? And in which year?

6. The first Live Aid concert, organised by Bob Geldof and Midge Ure in just 10 weeks, raised more than $100 million for famine relief in Africa. However, it was preceded by the Band Aid single *Do They Know It's Christmas?* which topped the Christmas charts soon after it was first released. In which year was this? Was it: a 1984
   b 1985
   c 1986

7. The punk band Sex Pistols was famous not just for its music but also for the anarchic personalities of its members, in particular Sid Vicious and Johnny Rotten. The band's second single, *God Save The Queen* was released in 1977 only to be immediately banned by Radio One. What royal event was Britain celebrating that year?

8. In 1967, after a tip-off, the police raided the country home of a member of the Rolling Stones, resulting in both he and another band member being given jail sentences – subsequently quashed on appeal – in relation to drugs. Whose home was it? The trial heard that there was just one woman in the house at the time – who was she?

9. The Supremes, consisting of Diana Ross, Mary Wilson and Florence Ballard, were one of the most successful musical acts of the 1960s. With which well-known record company were they signed? And in which year did Diana Ross give her last concert with what by then had become 'Diana Ross and the Supremes'?

10. In late 1996, America's *Newsweek* magazine called London the 'coolest capital city on the planet' and featured Oasis band member Liam Gallagher with his then partner British actress Patsy Kensit in bed covered by a Union Jack silk sheet. What popular phrase describing modern British society and culture was spawned by this media coverage?

The Sun
Wednesday August 17th 1977

Celebrities & Popular Culture – Part 2

1. On 4 July 1999, David Beckham, then footballer with Manchester United, married Victoria Adams, 'Posh Spice' from the famous girl band in a lavish ceremony which is said to have cost around £500,000 and united many stars from the world of football and show business. Name the place and the country where the wedding and the reception were held, and Beckham's best man.

2. Marilyn Monroe, born plain Norma Jean Baker, became a Hollywood icon and sex symbol in the 1950s thanks to films such as *Niagara*, *Gentlemen Prefer Blondes* and *The Seven Year Itch*. During this decade she married twice, on each occasion to men who were famous in their own right. Name them and their professions.

3. In 2005, *Forbes Magazine* estimated that the seemingly interminable series of Star Wars films had by then generated almost US$20billion in revenue, making it one of the most successful film franchises of all time. The first of the six films, called simply *Star Wars*, was first released in which year? Was it:
a 1974
b 1977
c 1979

4. In 1994 Elizabeth Hurley shot to fame when she appeared on the red carpet of a premiere wearing a sexy black dress that fastened with safety pins, by Italian designer Gianni Versace. She was attending the premiere of a film that starred her then boyfriend Hugh Grant. What was the name of the film and who wrote it?

5. What was the name coined by the media for the group of popular male performers, including Frank Sinatra, Sammy

Davis Junior and Dean Martin, who were credited with helping to desegregate Las Vegas hotels in the 1960s by refusing to play in those establishments that discriminated against Davis?

6. Which American artist first uttered the phrase, 'in the future everyone will be world famous for 15 minutes'? What is the name of the art movement to which he belonged? And what was the subject matter of his first solo exhibition in 1962?

7. At the end of 2005, civil partnerships between same-sex couples became legal in Great Britain. On the first day on which the law came into force, which celebrity couple celebrated their 'wedding' at Windsor Guildhall, a venue made royally famous a few months earlier?

8. Hollywood stars Elizabeth Taylor and Richard Burton made front-page news around the world when news of their affair broke; on the set of which blockbuster film did the pair meet and have an affair? And in which year did the pair famously get married – for the second time?

9. Walt Disney has become synonymous with some of the world's best-loved cartoon characters. In 1932, the Academy of Motion Picture Arts and Sciences presented Disney with an Oscar for the creation of which popular character, whose appearance in the 1928 hit animated film *Steamboat Willie* started to make him a household name?

10. JK Rowling's *Harry Potter* series has been so successful that the author has become one of the richest women in Britain – by 2003 her wealth had reportedly surpassed even that of the Queen. However, in March 2000 an English primary school head teacher announced she was banning the books. In which town was the school – and what reason did the teacher give for banning them?

The Sun
Tuesday July 6th 1999

Environment

1. An international conference on the subject of climate change and how to control it was held in Japan, which resulted in what is known as the Kyoto Protocol. In which year was this treaty negotiated and agreed, and which year did it officially come into force?

2. The disaster at the nuclear power station at Chernobyl in the Ukraine in 1986 killed thousands of people directly and caused serious long-term health problems for many more – its effects were felt as far away as Britain. However, the plant continued to produce electricity until it was finally shut down – in which year?

3. The shipwreck of the oil tanker *Torrey Canyon* off the south-west coast of England caused a major environmental disaster, though it was later claimed that the detergent used to clean the spillage killed more marine life than the oil. The authorities decided the best tactic was to sink the ship – how did they do this? And in which year did it happen?

4. An unusually cold winter and the subsequent increased burning of coal to provide heating helped cause the great smog that hit London from December 1952 to March 1953. The smog led to new legislation – what were the new laws called?

5. Though it was not on the scale of the Chernobyl disaster – no one immediately died from it – the United States had its own major nuclear energy accident in 1979. What was the name of the nuclear plant affected and which state is it in? And which film depicting a near meltdown at a nuclear power plant and featuring Jane Fonda was coincidentally on release at the time?

Disaster

6. Early in 2000 a spillage of cyanide from a gold smelter made its way through various waterways to the River Danube, en route killing huge numbers of fish and other wildlife. This environmental scandal made headlines all around the world. In which country did the cyanide spill occur?

7. The leaking of the *Exxon Valdez* super tanker in March 1989 was one of the worst oil-related environmental disasters in history. It killed tens of thousands of seabirds as well as seals, sea eagles and even killer whales. What is the name of the stretch of Alaskan coastline and water where the accident occurred?

8. In 1998 severely contaminated water threatened the wildlife of a Spanish national park and entered a river creating havoc for farmers, fish, birds and forests after a dam burst. What was the name of the river that was polluted and what was the nature of the industrial works from which the polluted water came?

9. Scandal hit New York State in the 1970s when it emerged that a residential area had been built on the site of an old chemical dump, from which various toxic chemicals had leaked and caused serious health problems. What was the name of the area affected – and which famous landmark is it near?

10. The rapid disappearance of much of the Amazonian rainforest has been a well-documented phenomenon in recent years. In 1988 it hit the headlines when a prominent Brazilian campaigner against the cutting down of trees to create cattle ranches was murdered. What was his name?

**The Independent
Thursday January 8th 2004**

Arts & Society

1. The publication of the novel *Lady Chatterley's Lover* by DH Lawrence was banned in Britain for many years because of its explicit scenes and language. In a famous court case the publishers finally won the right to publish the book on the grounds that it had literary and social merit. In which year was the court case and who were the publishers?

2. The opening of the tomb of the pharaoh Tutankhamen, discovered by archaeologist Howard Carter, was one of the most celebrated cultural events of the twentieth century. It also gave rise to stories about a curse after Carter's benefactor died. In which year was the tomb in the Valley of the Kings officially opened? And who was Carter's benefactor?

3. The great English writer George Orwell inspired many headlines even after his death, notably thanks to his novel *1984*, which foretells a future in which society is closely controlled by the authorities. What was the author's real name, and what is thought to have inspired his new surname?

4. The annual Prom concerts have been a feature of British musical life for more than a century, and have often attracted publicity. In September 2001 shortly after the terrorist attacks in New York and Washington D.C., the schedule of the Last Night of the Proms was adjusted to make way for a piece by an American composer. Which piece of music by which composer was played?

5. One of the best-known novels of the twentieth century, *Catch-22*, inspired a popular film of the same name which helped ensure that the expression became a fixture in the English language. Who wrote the novel and in which year was it published?

6. The famous Reading Room of the British Library has been used by many famous figures over the years, including Karl Marx, Charles Dickens and Virginia Woolf. However, the library has since moved from the British Museum to new premises at St Pancras. In which year did the Queen formally open the new purpose-built library?

7. The author Salman Rushdie brought the wrath of much of the Islamic world upon him when he published a controversial book that carried an irreverent depiction of the Prophet Muhammad. What was the name of the book, and in which year did Iranian leader Ayatollah Khomeini announce a fatwa calling for the death of Rushdie?

8. Until 1968 responsibility for the censorship of theatres lay in the hands of a senior official of the Royal Household and his office. What piece of legislation removed this outdated practice – and what was the title of the official concerned?

9. A controversial entry to the Turner Prize by a British artist was called *My Bed*, and consisted of an unmade bed. Who was that artist and in which year was the work short-listed for the prize?

10. The Nobel Prize for Literature is the greatest honour in the world of literature and is usually eagerly and gratefully received by the annual recipient. However in 1964 a writer and philosopher refused to accept the award, having apparently earlier tried to stop the judges awarding him the prize in the first place. Who was he?

Evening Standard
Wednesday November 2nd 1960

Olympics

1. The British rower Steve Redgrave entered the record books when he won his fifth consecutive Olympic gold medal at the Sydney games in 2000. As well the five golds, Redgrave also won an Olympic bronze in his career – in which year? And which debilitating condition did he suffer from in his latter years as a rower?

2. The first modern Olympic Games were staged in 1896, around fifteen centuries after they had been banned in Greece because of their pagan connections. Who was the man whose idea it was to revive the games and who became the first head of the International Olympic Committee?

3. The first modern games were held, appropriately enough, in Greece. One of the most keenly-awaited events was the marathon, which to the delight of the local population was won by an unknown Greek runner who overnight became a national hero and international celebrity. What was his name?

4. Women were not initially allowed to compete in the modern Olympics as, according to one senior official at the time, that would have been 'impractical, uninteresting, unaesthetic, and incorrect'. In which year did women compete for the first time? Was it:
a 1900
b 1904
c 1908

5. Female competitors were at the centre of controversy in 1928 when newspapers complained that the 800m competition that took place that year was too long for women. And after some competitors collapsed at the end of the race, the event was banned from the games, leaving the 200m as the longest race for women. In which year was the ban lifted?

6. At the Berlin Olympics in 1936 black American athlete Jesse Owens stole the headlines from Adolf Hitler and German athletes with a series of stunning performances. How many gold medals did Owens win and in which events?

7. The winter games are now a permanent fixture of the Olympic scene and are held two years after each summer games. However, the first winter games in 1924 were simply known at the time as an international 'winter sports week' and it was not until two years later that they were retroactively described as the first Winter Olympics. Where were they held?

8. American swimmer Mark Spitz swam into Olympic history in 1972 when at the Munich games he won seven golds: four in individual events and three in relays. In how many of the events did he also break or help break world records?

9. Though the Olympic Games are supposed to be free from politics, they have nonetheless become embroiled in political controversy on occasions. The most notable was the 1980 Moscow Games, boycotted by many nations and athletes – notably the US – though Britain did send a team despite the opposition of Margaret Thatcher's government. What was the reason for the boycott?

10. An ailing but proud Muhammad Ali carried the torch to light the Olympic flame and start the Atlanta games in 1996. Ali had himself won a boxing gold medal in the Olympics. In which year did he do so, and what did he later claim he had done with the medal?

The Daily Telegraph
Saturday September 23rd 2000

The Church and Religion

1. In 1981 Pope John Paul II survived a high-profile assassination attempt when a lone gunman shot him as he entered St Peter's Square in Rome. But in which year did a Spanish priest try to stab the pope with a bayonet? And in which place and country did this attempted assassination occur?

2. The Bishop of Durham caused consternation and outrage when he was widely quoted as likening the resurrection of Christ to a 'conjuring trick with bones'. In fact the bishop had simply been suggesting the opposite – that the resurrection could not be likened to such a trick. What was his name? And in which year did the row occur?

3. The Second Vatican Council – often referred to simply as Vatican II – was an important milestone in the Catholic Church, which among other outcomes permitted Mass to be said in the vernacular instead of Latin. Which pope called for the council, and in which year did it end?

4. The ordination of women into the priesthood in the Anglican Communion has taken place around the world for many years; indeed, a woman became a priest in Hong Kong in 1944. However, in which year did the Church of England finally approve the ordination of women to the priesthood, and in which year were the first women ordained?

5. In late 1959 a senior clerical figure was voted in as the first president of the soon to be independent island of Cyprus. Who was this high-profile cleric?

6. India was hit by unrest and violence in 1984 after the Indian Army besieged and took control of a Sikh holy site that was being held by Sikh militants; later that year Prime Minister Indira Gandhi was assassinated by two of her Sikh bodyguards. What is the name of the holy place and where is it located?

Clerical Error

7. In 1992 the then Bishop of Galway in Ireland was forced to resign his post – he went to work in South America – after it emerged he had had an affair with a woman and fathered a son by her. What was the name of that bishop and what was the nationality of his secret lover?

8. In 1985 a controversial church report on the state of Britain's inner cities and the plight of the poor set the Church of England on a collision course with the government of Margaret Thatcher, with one minister describing it as 'Marxist'. What was the name of the report?

9. The Tibetan spiritual leader the Dalai Lama was forced to flee his country after a crackdown by the authorities in China in response to a Tibetan rebellion. In which year did he permanently leave Tibet, in which country was he offered asylum, and when was he awarded the Nobel Peace Prize?

10. The return of Ayatollah Khomeini to Iran in 1979 after the Shah had been forced to flee marked the introduction of an Islamic Republic in the country. In which country had the Ayatollah spent the last few months of his exile before his triumphal return?

**Daily Mail
Thursday May 14th 1981**

Famous Firsts

1. The great American aviator Amelia Earhart captured the world's imagination when in 1928 she became the first woman to fly across the Atlantic Ocean. In 1937 she and her navigator vanished in mysterious circumstances while she sought to achieve another first. What was her aim?

2. The former trade union activist and campaigner for women's rights, Margaret Bondfield, became one of the first female MPs when she was elected to the House of Commons in 1923 as Labour MP for Northampton. Which notable first did she go on to achieve in 1929?

3. In July 1909 a French pioneer grabbed the headlines and made the British public suddenly aware that their country was not as remote – and safe – from the Continent as they had supposed. Who was he and what was his 'first'?

4. A former sailor in the Merchant and Royal Navy sailed into the record books in Falmouth in April 1969 when he became the first person to sail single-handed and non-stop around the world. In 1994, and with a co-skipper, he won the Jules Verne trophy for the fastest circumnavigation of the globe. Who was he?

5. Some of the most dramatic headlines in history greeted the news that Edmund Hillary had made it to the summit of Mount Everest in May 1953 – the first person to reach the peak of that famous mountain. What nationality was Hillary, what was his occupation – and what was the full name of the sherpa who was just a few paces behind him?

6. The first woman to swim across the English Channel was the American former Olympic swimmer Gertrude Ederle, who swam the distance in fourteen and a half hours – beating the previous record by men who had crossed the Channel by almost two hours and earning her a headline-grabbing ticker-tape parade back in New York. In which year did she achieve this?

a 1924
b 1926
c 1932

7. The world's first woman minister took office in 1960 in Asia; by the time of her death in 2000 this woman had in fact been prime minister of her country no fewer than three times. Which country was it – and what was her name?

8. When in 1966 Robert Weaver was appointed by US President Lyndon Johnson as president of the new Department of Housing and Urban Development, it marked a significant milestone in American society and politics. What was that milestone?

9. When the United Nations was created in 1945 it replaced the old and discredited League of Nations that had been unable to stop mounting international tension in the 1930s. In 1946 the UN got its first General Secretary; who was he and what was his nationality?

10. Some people considered it was impossible to run a mile in under four minutes, so when student Roger Bannister achieved this feat in Oxford in May 1954 it made headlines all around the world. What was Bannister studying and who were his two pacemakers in this race against the clock?

**Daily Mirror
Tuesday June 19th 1928**

Soviet Union

1. The abdication of Tsar Nicolas II in early 1917 marked the first of two revolutions in Russia that year, culminating in the Bolsheviks coming to power in the autumn and ultimately the creation of the Soviet Union. Who was the prime minister of the so-called Provisional Government when the communists then seized power in October?

2. Though the communists took power in Russia in 1917, a bloody civil war ensued involving the so-called White Russians fighting against the communist or Red Russians. This conflict effectively ended when the leading White Russian general had to evacuate his troops in November 1920. What was the name of this general?

3. The death of the Soviet leader Vladimir Lenin marked the passing of the man who was most instrumental in bringing the Bolsheviks to power in Russia. His name was a pseudonym: what was Lenin's real name and in which year did he die?

4. Another key figure in the creation of the Soviet Union was the intellectual Leon Trotsky, who led the Red Army during the civil war. However, after Lenin's death he went into exile before he was eventually murdered. In which year and country did he die, and what implement was used to kill him?

5. The man who eventually replaced Lenin as the key figure in the Soviet Union was Joseph Stalin, who became effective dictator from the late 1920s. What nationality was he, in what kind of establishment had he been educated as a young man – and what does his nickname Stalin mean?

6. The Battle of Stalingrad in World War Two, in which Soviet defenders managed to repulse and eventually destroy the German attack, is often seen as a major turning point in the war. However the city was renamed in 1961; what did it become and on which river does it stand?

7. The famous speech given by Winston Churchill in which he noted how an 'iron curtain has descended...' across Europe described the process by which Stalin's Soviet Union had extended its influence into Eastern Europe by effectively controlling the governments of those countries. From where to where did Churchill say this iron curtain ran?

8. The death of Stalin in 1953 allowed criticism of the dictator and his bloody rule to emerge gradually in Soviet society, though he had been portrayed as a Soviet hero and even as a kind of demigod in the past. Who eventually replaced him as the new Soviet leader and in which year was Stalin's body symbolically removed from Lenin's Tomb?

9. Leonid Brezhnev presided over the Soviet Union in the 1970s at a time when the Soviet system seemed increasingly old-fashioned and out of step with the modern world. When he died in 1982 he was followed in quick succession by two other short-lived leaders. Who were they?

10. The Soviet leader Mikhail Gorbachev presided over policies that were to lead to the end of communist rule in the old Iron Curtain European countries. Hardliners who feared the end of the Soviet Union staged a coup attempt and briefly held Gorbachev captive. In which year was this and where was the Soviet leader at the time?

The Daily Chronicle
Friday March 16th 1917

Middle East

1. After the war between Israel and her Arab neighbours in 1967 the former took control of land that would be at the centre of the Israeli-Palestinian crisis for many years to come. What is the usual name given to this war? One of the territories gained by Israel was the Sinai Peninsula – what were the others?

2. The Sinai Peninsula was eventually returned to Egyptian hands after a treaty between Israel and Egypt – the first such treaty between Israel and her Arab neighbours. In which year did this occur and who were the respective leaders of the two countries?

3. The so-called Balfour Declaration signalled British Government support for the 'establishment in Palestine of a national home for the Jewish people' though it was added that this must not prejudice the rights of other communities in Palestine. In what year was this declaration made and what position did Arthur Balfour hold?

4. The state of Israel was created in 1948 following a United Nations resolution that divided the area then known as Palestine into a Jewish state and a Palestinian state, though immediately the new Israeli nation was at war with its neighbours. Who became the first Israeli prime minister?

5. The death of Yasser Arafat in 2004 marked the end of an era in the Middle East; for many years he had been the living symbol of the Palestinian cause. In which year had he first become chairman of the executive committee of the Palestinian Liberation Organisation? In which country did he die?

6. During the late 1970s and 1980s Lebanon and its capital Beirut became synonymous with disorder, instability and violence during a civil war that included intervention by both Syria and Israel. In which year did Israel invade Lebanon, in

Conflict

which year did the civil war there begin – and in which year did it officially end?

7. The Middle Eastern country of Qatar, which was formerly a British protectorate, has become a major source of the world's gas supplies and in 1997 became the host country of an important new TV station. In which year did Qatar become independent and what is the name of the TV company?

8. In the late 1940s a series of ancient parchments including Biblical texts were discovered in caves near the ancient city of Qumran in the area now known as the West Bank. By what name are these parchments generally known? And a member of which traditionally nomadic people is credited with their discovery?

9. The pilgrimage or Haj that Muslims make to Mecca in Saudi Arabia has led to several tragedies. In the worst incident in recent times 1,426 pilgrims were killed – mostly suffocated or trampled to death as thousands made their way through a tunnel. In which year did this happen?

10. When King Hussein of Jordan died it marked the end of one of the longest ruling leaders in the Middle East. In which year did he die, what is the name of his fourth wife and widow, and what is the official name of the dynasty that rules in Jordan?

The Evening News and Star
Monday June 5th 1967

Explorers & Exploration

1. News that the explorer Roald Amundsen had become the first man to reach the South Pole flashed around the world in March 1912, though he had actually achieved the feat back in December 1911. What nationality was Amundsen and how many other explorers were with him on this historic venture?

2. Amundsen famously beat the British explorer Robert Scott to the South Pole by a month. Scott and his four companions then perished in the Antarctic wastes as they made their way back from the Pole, though their diaries were found. Which team member's famous last words were: 'I am just going outside – and may be some time'?

3. A fellow explorer of Scott's was Ernest Shackleton who became best known for heroically leading his team to safety after a later, failed expedition to the South Pole that began in 1914. What was the name of his ship that got stuck in the ice, and what was the aim of the expedition?

4. The British explorer and mountaineer George Mallory and his climbing companion Andrew Irvine perished while attempting to climb Mount Everest. In which year did they die, in which year was Mallory's body found – and what famous reason did he reportedly give for wanting to climb the mountain?

5. During a three-year global trek that ended in 1982 a well-known British explorer succeeded in becoming the first man to reach both poles by land. What is the explorer's name?

6. In 1993 Ann Bancroft led the first women's team to reach the South Pole using skis and sleds and by doing so she became the first woman to reach both poles across the ice. What nationality is she?

7. The British explorer and adventurer David Hempleman-Adams became the first person to reach the geomagnetic North Pole alone and unsupported – though he had not told his wife what he was about to do. In which year did he achieve this feat and what had he told his family he was going to do?

8. The person generally credited with having been the first man to lead an expedition to the North Pole was an American explorer and naval officer, even if some people have subsequently doubted whether, because of navigational errors, the group actually made it all the way to the pole. What was the man's name and in which year did he reach the North Pole?

9. The underwater explorer Robert Ballard made headlines around the world when he discovered the most famous shipwreck in history – the *Titanic*. In which year did he locate the ship? Was it:
a 1985
b 1986
c 1987

10. Though Sir Edmund Hillary is best known for his exploits on Mount Everest, he was also a noted explorer and led a high-profile expedition to reach the South Pole. In which year did this occur; and which British explorer arrived soon afterwards to join Sir Edmund at the South Pole?

The Daily Chronicle
Saturday March 9th 1912

Space Exploration

1. The first human went into space on 12 April 1961, making a one-orbit journey around the Earth in his space vessel. According to media reports at the time, this pioneering cosmonaut Yuri Gagarin was quoted as saying, 'I don't see any god up here.' What was the name of his spacecraft and how did Gagarin die in 1968?

2. American Neil Armstrong became the first man to walk on the Moon when he placed his left foot onto its surface on 21 July 1969. What is the name given to the area of the Moon onto which he first stepped, and what famous words did he utter?

3. Before humans, many different animals went into space, most famously a rhesus monkey called Able and a South American squirrel monkey named Baker. These were the first animals to survive a space flight, landing safely in 1959. What, though, were the first living creatures sent into space, to test the effect of radiation?

4. Launched in 1990, a telescope put into orbit around the Earth has become one of the most important astronomical tools of the modern age, responsible for many ground-breaking observations. What is the name of the telescope, after whom was it named, and what nationality was he?

5. Humans have long speculated whether the so-called Red Planet – Mars – could sustain life and many attempts have been made to send spacecraft to it. In which year did a space probe land on that planet's surface for the first time? Which country sent it?

6. The Soviet Union's launch in October 1957 of the first artificial Earth satellite marked the beginning of the space race between the USSR and USA. What was its name? And what was the name of the first US satellite launched months later?

Rocket Man

7. Valentina Tereshkova, then aged 26, was the first woman in space, orbiting the Earth 48 times in Vostok 6. In which year did she go into space? Was it:
a 1963
b 1968
c 1973

8. The first reusable spacecraft was launched by NASA, and a total of five have now flown beyond Earth's atmosphere. Officially part of the Space Transportation System, this space vehicle is more commonly known by which term? In which year was the first one launched?

9. The International Space Station is a joint project between five space agencies. As well as being responsible for scientific experimentation, it has become the focus of which recent and more frivolous space phenomenon, the first example occurring in April 2001 at a cost of US$20million?

10. In 1977 two unmanned probes blasted off from the Earth on a voyage that would take them to the giant planets Saturn and Jupiter and in the case of one of them past Uranus and Neptune too. One of the probes is now the farthest human-made object from the Earth and like its sister ship continues to travel far into deep space. What are their names?

Daily Mirror
Thursday April 13th 1961

Science

1. The announcement in 2000 that scientists had succeeded in mapping nearly all of the human body's genetic code or DNA was hailed as one of the most important scientific milestones in history. What was the name of the project that co-ordinated this global scientific effort, and when was it finally completed?

2. When the physicist and mathematician Albert Einstein died in 1955, the then US President Dwight Eisenhower said of him: 'No other man contributed so much to the vast expansion of twentieth-century knowledge.' In which year did Einstein publish his ground-breaking Special Theory of Relativity and in which year was he awarded the Nobel Prize for Physics?

3. In 1911 Marie Curie won the second of her two Nobel Prizes for her work on radioactivity, making her the most famous and acclaimed woman scientist in history. In which country was she born, and what was the first name of her husband with whom she had shared her 1903 Nobel prize?

4. It was announced in 1997 that a sheep had been cloned, making her the first mammal to have been successfully produced in this way from an adult cell. What was the name of this sheep, what was the name of the research centre where she was 'created', and in what country was it?

5. In 1945 a leading scientist watched the testing of the world's first atomic bomb that he had helped to develop and then declared: 'I am become Death, the destroyer of worlds.' What was his name and what was the name of the US project to develop the bomb?

6. The theoretical physicist Stephen Hawking wrote an acclaimed book called *A Brief History of Time* that despite being about the most complex of subjects sold millions of copies. In which year was it published?

Miracle

7. During a BBC radio broadcast in 1950 a British astronomer coined the term 'Big Bang' to describe a theory about how the universe began; ironically, though this name has stuck ever since, the astronomer himself never agreed with the theory and used the term scornfully. What was his name and what was the name of the alternative theory he supported?

8. In 1989 two chemists at the University of Utah announced they had succeeded in an apparently simple experiment in creating what was potentially a revolutionary breakthrough in producing cheap and safe energy. Who were the scientists and what was the name of the process they claimed to have demonstrated?

9. An internationally-acclaimed scientist resigned from his university late in 2005 after it emerged that some of the results of his breakthrough research into stem cells had apparently been fabricated. Which nationality was this scientist and what was his name?

10. In 2004 the discovery of a new large mass beyond the ninth planet Pluto in our Solar System was announced; some described it as a 'planetoid'; others suggested it was in fact the tenth planet in our system. What was the name given to this new 'planet' by its discoverers, and where did the name come from?

The Mirror
Tuesday June 27th 2000

Medicine

1. On 25 July 1978, Louise Joy Brown, the world's first baby born from *in vitro* fertilisation, was delivered by a planned caesarean section in Britain and made front page news all around the world. Name either one of the two doctors responsible for this first successful use of IVF. Where did the birth take place?

2. It has been called the most devasting epidemic in recorded world history, and was estimated to have killed between 50 million and 100 million people from 1918–1919 – far more than died in combat in the First World War. A deadly strain of avian flu, by what name was it commonly known at the time?

3. The first British public health campaign warning about the dangers of HIV/AIDS bore the slogan 'Don't Aid AIDS' and was not generally considered to have been very effective. In which year was it launched?

4. The contraceptive pill for women is considered to have played a major role in the emancipation of women. In which year was it first made available in the UK and who was the health minister who announced that the pill would be available on the NHS?

5. In 1905 Englishman Dr William Fletcher found that eating unpolished rice prevented beriberi while eating polished rice did not, so making the discovery that food contained different nutritional elements. Seven years later, Polish scientist Cashmir Funk gave them a name. What was this now widely-used name?

6. A surgeon performed the first heart transplant on 53-year-old Lewis Washkansky, on 3 December 1967. Though the surgery was a success, and his heart continued to beat strongly right to the end, the patient died of double pneumonia 18 days later. In which country was the transplant carried out? Who was the surgeon?

Breakthrough

7. Originally discovered in 1896 by a young French scientist, penicillin was largely ignored until Scottish scientist Ian Fleming realised its antibiosis effect 32 years later in 1928. It was not widely used, however, until its chemical structure was determined – enabling it to be produced synthetically. Who was responsible for this crucial discovery?

8. In the 1950s and 60s, the drug thalidomide was prescribed to pregnant women primarily to alleviate morning sickness. However, it was later exposed as being the cause of severe birth defects. Which British newspaper ran a long-running investigation and campaign to highlight this issue? Who was its editor at the time?

9. 'Sildenafil citrate' is the pharmaceutical name of a drug first patented amid many titillating headlines in 1998, and which is used to treat erectile dysfunction, as well as pulmonary arterial hypertension. What is the drug's more commonly used name? And which pharmaceutical company introduced it?

10. In 2005 surgeons in France carried out a pioneering transplant on a woman who had been savaged by a dog. The operation took five hours and used different parts of a donor who was brain-dead. Which part of the woman's body was replaced?

Evening News
Thursday July 27th 1978

Answers

Political Scandals
1. 'The trusty shield of British fair play'
2. Aitken said his wife Lolicia had paid the bill at the Ritz hotel
3. Mark Felt, number two in the FBI, whose identity was revealed by *Vanity Fair* magazine
4. Nicaragua; Lt-Col Oliver North
5. Senator Edward Kennedy drove the car in which Mary Jo Kopechne was killed in 1969
6. The novelist Émile Zola, who entitled his letter 'J'accuse!'
7. Hugh Dalton
8. Lord Kagan, who was a raincoat manufacturer
9. Leon Brittan, Trade and Industry Secretary
10. Fellow Labour MP Geoffrey Robinson

Sex Scandals
1. Secretary of State for Trade and Industry; Flora
2. Kimberly Quinn (or Kimberly Fortier) was Publisher of *The Spectator*; her nanny was from the Philippines
3. Kenneth Starr
4. a 1994
5. Lord Denning, Master of the Rolls
6. 1992; 1999
7. Heidi Fleiss
8. Chelsea FC; Max Clifford
9. Jimmy Swaggart
10. Gaynor Regan was Cook's secretary; Margaret

Financial Disasters and Scandals
1. b Herbert Hoover
2. Singapore

3. In the Atlantic Ocean, off the Canary Islands
4. A violent storm, often referred to as the Great Storm
5. The Dot-Com Crash
6. John Poulson
7. Polly Peck; Turkish Cyprus
8. Ernest Saunders, Anthony Parnes and Gerald Ronson
9. Norman Lamont; his bathroom
10. Bank of Credit and Commerce International (BCCI); Pakistani

Rail and Road Disasters
1. Paul Channon
2. Modane in France
3. Moorgate
4. Russia; 1989
5. They were all women
6. A discarded match
7. Salisbury, Wiltshire
8. Mont Blanc
9. c Afghanistan
10. Lord Cullen

Air Disasters
1. Most died from jumping or falling to the ground when the airship caught fire
2. 1985; Greece
3. Uruguay
4. Golfer Payne Stewart
5. Charles de Gaulle, Paris
6. The Mull of Kintyre
7. Red Star Belgrade
8. Tenerife; KLM and Pan Am
9. Secretary of State for Air; Karachi
10. The Ukraine

Nautical Disasters
1. Unlawful killing; Dover
2. Queenstown (now Cobh), Ireland

3. c 2000
4. Fastnet race
5. MS *Estonia*; Sweden
6. It collided with an oil tanker
7. The *Lusitania* was torpedoed on 7 May 1915, with the loss of more than 1,100 lives
8. *Bowbelle*, a dredger
9. a Senegal
10. *Gaul*; Hull

Space Disasters
1. b 1988
2. Russian. Soviet cosmonaut Vladimir Komarov was killed on impact aboard Soyuz 1 on 24 April 1967 when it returned to earth
3. A fire – their capsule was set alight by an electrical fault
4. 1970
5. Colin Pillinger; Beagle 2; HMS *Beagle*, the ship on which Charles Darwin sailed
6. One team had used metric units while the other used imperial measures
7. A dog named Laika
8. *Columbia*
9. China; the Long March 3B rocket had taken off from Xichang space centre
10. They spent the night surrounded by wolves in a remote part of the Ural Mountains

Chemical and Fire Disasters
1. Piper Alpha; Occidental Oil
2. c 1974
3. Union Carbide; 1984
4. They had just been presented with the Third

Division Championship trophy, having won promotion to the second division
5. A spotlight shining on a curtain and igniting it
6. New Cross, south-east London
7. Dr David Jenkins; Bishop of Durham
8. Buncefield
9. Coconut Grove; Buck Jones
10. Toulouse; chemical fertiliser plant

Royal Family – Part 1
1. Stanley Baldwin; Conservative Party
2. Warfield
3. Treetops Hotel, Kenya
4. c 1992
5. 1976; Montreal
6. 1958
7. HMS *Bronington*; 1976
8. Prince Edward
9. 1997
10. Bowes-Lyon; 1993

Royal Family – Part 2
1. a 1992
2. Martin Bashir; *Panorama*; Camilla Parker Bowles
3. RAF Northolt, west London; the Royal Standard
4. 1974; her then husband Captain Mark Phillips
5. Michael Fagan; 1982; stealing half a bottle of wine
6. Sir Laurens van der Post; South Africa
7. Albert; Duke of York
8. The documentary *Royal Family*
9. Prince Charles' polo manager; major; 2003
10. Klosters

Natural Disasters
1. The Netherlands
2. 1999
3. Iran
4. b 1974
5. The Long Island Express

(also the Great New England Hurricane)
6. Opera singer Plácido Domingo
7. Lynmouth; 1952
8. c fifteen million
9. Australia
10. 1976

Killers
1. Wireless telegraphy; the ship's captain wired ahead that Crippen was on board
2. Ted Bundy; Florida; the electric chair
3. Thomas Hamilton; 1996
4. Hyde, Greater Manchester; 2004
5. Lorry driver
6. Columbine High School; Colorado
7. Cromwell Street; Gloucester
8. 10 Rillington Place
9. Saddleworth Moor, near Manchester
10. 1987

Assassinations & Assassination Attempts
1. They claimed he had betrayed the cause of Hindus and Hindu India in agreeing to the partition of India and Pakistan
2. b 1979
3. Memphis, Tennessee; 1968
4. Turkish; Virgin Mary of Fatima
5. Three: Presidents Lincoln, Garfield and McKinley
6. 1984 & 1991
7. Actress Jodie Foster
8. Granting independence to the French colony of Algeria
9. Los Angeles; Sirhan Sirhan
10. 1995; Tel Aviv

Ireland
1. Gordon and Marie Wilson
2. a 1916

3. The Ulster Volunteer Force (UVF)
4. 1969; Major James Chichester-Clark
5. Drumcree Parish Church, Drumcree
6. Lord Widgery; Lord Saville
7. 1949
8. Michael Stone
9. Bobbie Sands; the Maze
10. 1998

Espionage
1. Surveyor of the Queen's Pictures, making him Her Majesty's art adviser; 1979; Prime Minister Margaret Thatcher
2. The Cambridge Apostles
3. 1963
4. France; 1917
5. Violette Szabo
6. John Walker
7. c 1999
8. Head of West German counter-intelligence
9. The East German secret police the Stasi; CND
10. Julius and Ethel Rosenberg; 1953

Labour Disputes
1. Miners; nine
2. a 1936
3. baseball
4. 1986; News International
5. Gravediggers
6. Grunwick
7. February; Harold Wilson
8. Orgreave; March 1985
9. 1968
10. Liverpool; Derek Hatton

World War One
1. Ypres
2. Herbert Asquith; Liberal Party; David Lloyd George
3. a 1914
4. Douglas Haig
5. Baghdad; the Ottomans
6. Airships, usually known as Zeppelins
7. Dardanelles Straits
8. Battle of Jutland

9. Manfred von Richthofen;
   the 'Red Baron'; 1918
10. The Treaty of Versailles

Hitler
1. Austria; 1889
2. Lance corporal
3. Beer Hall Putsch
4. The Brownshirts; The
   Night of the Long Knives
5. c 1933
6. *Mein Kampf*; *My Struggle*
7. Eva Braun; Heinrich
   Hoffmann, who became
   Hitler's official
   photographer
8. Wolf's Lair
9. July 20 Plot or July Plot
10. He shot himself

Appeasement
1. 1937; 1940
2. 'Peace for our time...'
3. The Sudetenland
4. Anthony Eden; Lord
   Halifax
5. Edvard Benes
6. Anschluss; March 1938
7. Stanley Baldwin
8. The League of Nations
9. March 1939
10. Oliver Cromwell, 1653

World War Two– Part 1
1. The Phoney War
2. Finland
3. The British
   Expeditionary Force
4. July; October
5. Operation Sealion
6. June 1941; Operation
   Barbarossa
7. Oahu; December 1941
8. Battleship *Prince of Wales*;
   battlecruiser *Repulse*
9. Greece
10. Hendaye, France

World War Two – Part 2
1. To destroy it
2. General Dwight D
   Eisenhower; Operation
   Overlord
3. Field Marshal Erwin
   Rommel; The Desert Fox;
   The Afrika Korps
4. William Joyce
5. Maquis

6. Stalingrad; 6th Army
7. c Milan
8. Marshal Georgi Zhukov;
   Admiral Karl Dönitz
9. Enola Gay
10. President Harry S
    Truman; Winston
    Churchill then Clement
    Attlee after Labour's
    election win on July 26

Churchill
1. St Paul's Cathedral; by
   lowering their cranes
2. John Churchill, First
   Duke of Marlborough
3. War correspondent; the
   Boer War
4. Liberal Party
5. First Lord of the
   Admiralty; fighting on
   the Western Front
6. Clementine Hozier;
   Chartwell
7. The return of Britain to
   the gold standard
8. First Lord of the
   Admiralty
9. British victory at El
   Alamein in 1942
10. Nobel Prize for
    Literature

International Crises/Cold War – Part 1
1. He had nationalised the
   company that ran the
   canal
2. 1948
3. Nikita Khrushchev and
   John F Kennedy; 1962
4. Dien Bien Phu
5. a 1968
6. Hutus and Tutsis
7. Bangladesh, formerly
   East Pakistan
8. It was a UN safe haven
   or safe area; 1995
9. Belgium; 1960
10. The cruiser *General
    Belgrano*; the nuclear
    powered submarine HMS
    Conqueror

International Crises/Cold War – Part 2
1. 1953
2. Kim Il Sung; 1994; his

son Kim Jong Il
3. Gary Powers
4. Pieds-noirs
5. A lone student standing
   in front of a line of
   tanks; 1989
6. Nigeria
7. 1980
8. Khmer Rouge;
   Kampuchea
9. Michael Buerk
10. 1961; Checkpoint
    Charlie; Erich Honecker

Landmark British Political Events – Part 1
1. Clement Attlee; six
   years, until 1951
2. The Beveridge Report
3. 1911; Herbert Asquith
4. 1922
5. 1924; Ramsay
   MacDonald
6. Devaluation of the pound
   in 1967
7. Harold Macmillan; 1962
8. Birmingham; Defence
   spokesman in
   Conservative Shadow
   Cabinet
9. Denmark, Ireland;
   Belgium, France, Italy,
   Luxembourg, Holland
   and West Germany
10. Baron Wilson of
    Rievaulx; James
    Callaghan

Landmark British Political Events – Part 2
1. Sir Anthony Meyer; Sir
   Geoffrey Howe
2. Abolished free school
   milk; 'Maggie Thatcher,
   milk snatcher'
3. c 1983
4. Limehouse Declaration;
   Roy Jenkins, Dr David
   Owen, Shirley Williams
   and William Rodgers
5. 1988; Paddy Ashdown
6. Sheffield
7. Margaret Beckett
8. Granita; Islington
9. 1979
10. 2000; Tony Blair's father

Sporting Achievements
1. Azerbaijan
2. Hampden Park, Glasgow; five times
3. The Oval; nought; Eric Hollies
4. 1980; John McEnroe; US Open
5. a 1930
6. Juan Manuel Fangio; Argentinian
7. 1995; Donald 'Ginger' McCain
8. 1967; Inter Milan; Portugal
9. 17–20; France
10. Simon Jones; Kevin Pietersen

Sporting Controversies
1. Harold Larwood and Bill Voce; England 4–1
2. Charlton Athletic
3. 1978
4. Port Vale
5. Trevor; New Zealand
6. Sheffield Wednesday
7. 99; Willie John McBride
8. Jean-Marc Bosman; R.F.C. de Liège
9. 2000; India
10. Robert Hoyzer

Social Protests and Unrest
1. Emily Wilding Davison; 1913; 1918
2. Aldermaston
3. Lord Scarman; Toxteth
4. 1990; 1991; Community charge
5. Mods and Rockers
6. Fathers 4 Justice
7. Rodney King; 1992
8. The March for Liberty and Livelihood
9. Mink; New Forest
10. Auckland; Laurent Fabius

Television – History and Programmes
1. Alexandra Palace
2. John Reith; British Broadcasting Company
3. 1938
4. Toothpaste; *The Archers* – death of Grace Archer
5. *Telstar*

6. 1967; BBC2; David Attenborough
7. c 1955
8. Jeremy Isaacs
9. Sir John Betjeman; Tony Warren
10. TV-am; Roland Rat

Celebrities & Popular Culture – Part 1
1. Cardiac arrhythmia, or a 'severely irregular heartbeat'; on the bathroom floor of his multi-million-dollar Graceland Mansion
2. *Thriller*; 1982
3. *American Pie*; 1972
4. Madonna Louise Ciccone; Detroit; Guy Richie
5. John Lennon; 1966
6. a 1984
7. It was the Queen's Silver Jubilee
8. Keith Richards; Marianne Faithful
9. Motown Records; 1970
10. Cool Britannia

Celebrities & Popular Culture – Part 2
1. Luttrellstown Castle near Dublin in Ireland; footballer Gary Neville
2. Joe DiMaggio, baseball player & Arthur Miller, playwright
3. b 1977
4. *Four Weddings and A Funeral*; Richard Curtis
5. The Rat Pack
6. Andy Warhol; Pop Art; Campbell's Soup Cans
7. Elton John and David Furnish
8. *Cleopatra*; 1975
9. Mickey Mouse
10. Chatham, Kent; she said they went against Bible teaching

Environment
1. 1997; 2005
2. 2000
3. The RAF and Navy bombed it; 1967
4. The Clean Air Acts

5. Three Mile Island; Pennsylvania; China Syndrome
6. Romania
7. Prince William Sound
8. Guadiamar; iron pyrite mine
9. Love Canal; Niagara Falls
10. Francisco Alves Mendes Filho, better known as Chico Mendes

Arts & Society
1. 1960; Penguin
2. 1923; Lord Carnarvon
3. Eric Blair; the River Orwell in Suffolk
4. Adagio for Strings; Samuel Barber
5. Joseph Heller; 1961
6. 1998
7. *The Satanic Verses*; 1989
8. Theatres Act 1968; the Lord Chamberlain
9. Tracey Emin; 1999
10. French writer and thinker Jean-Paul Sartre

Olympics
1. 1988; diabetes
2. Pierre de Coubertin
3. Spiridon Louis
4. a 1900
5. 1960
6. Four; 100m, 200m, 4x100m and long jump
7. Chamonix, France
8. seven
9. The Soviet invasion of Afghanistan in 1979
10. 1960; he said he threw it in a river after being refused service at an all-white diner

The Church and Religion
1. 1982; Fatima, Portugal
2. David Jenkins; 1984
3. Pope John XXIII; 1965
4. 1992; 1994
5. Archbishop Makarios
6. Golden Temple; Amritsar
7. Eamon Casey; American
8. Faith in the City
9. 1959; India; 1989
10. France

Famous Firsts

1. To be the first woman to fly around the world
2. First female Cabinet minister in Britain
3. Louis Blériot became the first person to fly an aeroplane across the English Channel
4. Robin (later Sir) Knox-Johnston
5. New Zealander; beekeeper; Tenzing Norgay
6. b 1926
7. Sri Lanka; Sirimavo Bandaranaike
8. He became the US's first black Cabinet member
9. Trygve Lie; Norwegian
10. Medicine; Chris Brasher and Chris Chataway

Soviet Union

1. Alexander Kerensky
2. Baron Piotr Wrangel
3. Vladimir Ilyich Ulyanov; 1924
4. 1940; Mexico; an ice-pick
5. Georgian; seminary; 'man of steel'
6. Volgograd; Volga
7. From 'Stettin in the Baltic to Trieste in the Adriatic'
8. Nikita Khrushchev; 1961
9. Yuri Andropov and Konstantin Chernenko
10. 1991; in a dacha in the Crimea

Middle East

1. Six Day War; Sinai; Gaza Strip; Golan Heights; West Bank, including East Jerusalem
2. 1979; Israeli Prime Minister Menachem Begin and President Anwar al-Sadat of Egypt
3. 1917; Arthur Balfour was British Foreign Secretary
4. David Ben-Gurion
5. 1969; France
6. 1982; 1975; 1990
7. 1971; Al-Jazeera TV
8. Dead Sea Scrolls; Bedouin
9. 1990
10. 1999; Queen Noor; the Hashemite dynasty

Explorers & Exploration

1. Norwegian; four
2. Captain Lawrence Oates
3. *Endurance*; to be the first to cross the polar continent
4. 1924; 1999; 'because it is there'
5. Sir Ranulph Fiennes
6. American
7. 2003; 'go skiing in the Arctic'
8. Robert Peary; 1909
9. a 1985
10. 1958; Sir Vivian Fuchs

Space Exploration

1. *Vostok 1*; his jet aircraft crashed during a training flight
2. Sea of Tranquility; 'That's one small step for man but one giant leap for mankind.'
3. Fruit flies
4. The Hubble Space Telescope; astronomer Edwin Hubble; American
5. 1971; Soviet Union
6. *Sputnik 1*; *Explorer 1* (or satellite 1958 Alpha)
7. a 1963
8. Space Shuttle; 1981
9. Space tourism – the first 'guest' was American businessman Dennis Tito
10. *Voyager 1* and *Voyager 2*

Science

1. Human Genome Project; 2003
2. 1905; 1921
3. Poland; Pierre
4. Dolly; Roslin Institute; Scotland
5. J Robert Oppenheimer; Manhattan Project
6. 1988
7. Sir Fred Hoyle; steady state theory
8. Stanley Pons and Martin Fleischmann; cold nuclear fusion
9. Korean; Hwang Woo-Suk
10. Sedna; the Inuit goddess of the ocean

Medicine

1. Dr Patrick Steptoe and Dr Robert Edwards; Oldham and District General Hospital, Greater Manchester
2. Spanish Flu Pandemic; also La Grippe
3. 1987
4. 1961; Enoch Powell
5. Vitamine – later changed to vitamin
6. South Africa, Christiaan Barnard
7. Dorothy Crowfoot Hodgkin
8. *The Sunday Times*; Harold Evans
9. Viagra; Pfizer
10. her face